MATH ^{GRADE}3 WARM-UPS

Developing Fluency In Math

Written by **Sheri Disbrow** ✎ Illustrated by **Stephanie O'Shaughnessy**

Edited by **Dianne Draze** and Chandra K Smith

Published by Prufrock Press Inc.

ISBN 1-59363-104-9

For more information about our products, visit our website
http://www.prufrock.com

Introduction

Do You Need Another Math Book?

If you already use a basal text, do you really need another math book? For most teachers, the answer is "yes." This supplementary math book reinforces the concepts presented in basal texts, giving additional, consistent review of the most important math concepts that are presented at this grade level. Even teachers who use a basal text will find it necessary to give additional practice to assure that students have a concrete grasp of mathematical concepts. *Math Warm-Ups* is challenging and integrates a variety of content in each lesson. It gradually increases in difficulty, making it the perfect math supplement.

Math Warm-Ups and Math Standards

This is one in a series of supplementary math text books. Each book is a daily math workbook, designed to meet math standards for a specific grade level. This book was developed according to the national, Ohio, California, and Texas content standards and objectives for third grade.

Each page of *Math Warm-Ups* offers ten problems that deal with a variety of concepts. The problems address the following math standards:

- understand the meaning of addition and subtraction
- compute fluently and make estimates
- recognize and extend patterns
- name and draw two- and three-dimensional shapes
- apply transformations
- measure using various units or systems
- represent data in pictures and graphs
- analyze data
- apply appropriate strategies to solve problems
- use the language of mathematics to express mathematical ideas.

What's So Great About This Book?

This book consistently exposes students to a variety of concepts in all objective areas, including common sense. It is quick and easy for the teacher to grade and provides immediate and repeated opportunities for re-teaching. *Math Warm-Ups* is designed to aid the teacher in covering all objectives and provides the students with opportunities to practice several math objectives on a regular basis. It stimulates learning and encourages the use of different problem solving techniques. The advantages of using this text are that it:

- is easy to grade
- motivates students
- provides daily diagnosis of students' weaknesses
- covers a variety of objectives
- spirals in level of difficulty
- consistently builds critical thinking and problem solving skills
- addresses problem solving daily in small pieces
- combines multiple objectives into several questions
- presents multi-step problems
- asks open ended questions
- supports the existing curriculum
- eliminates "holes" in learning, thus enabling students to meet standards
- can be used individually or with a whole class
- provides a quick diagnosis of new students' abilities
- addresses multiple objectives within a five-day period
- enables productive parent conferences, pinpointing problem areas
- assists teachers in finding weak areas where additional instructional focus is needed.

How to Use the Book

This workbook is can be used in a variety of ways. It can be used as a warm-up, as homework, or as a diagnostic tool. You can use it as a daily or weekly review or as additional practice to supplement your regular math instruction.

Teachers, parents, and administrators can use this workbook to diagnose weak areas and also to ensure the conceptual understanding of the students on a daily basis. Parents, students, and teachers can evaluate progress, which will allow them to identify and correct deficiencies. It empowers students and motivates them to invest in their own learning. Parents who want to make sure that their children have mastered math skills and will be ready for any testing situation will find this workbook thorough and easy to use. Additionally, teachers who want to provide individual practice for students who are ready to move faster through the curriculum can use these exercises and be comfortable that students are getting practice in a broad spectrum of math skills.

The **Math Warm-Ups** series came out of a need to ensure students' success while developing mathematical thinkers and problem solvers. It has been tested and used in the classroom with great success. Students who use these exercises are interested and motivated because they are given repeated opportunities to be successful. Practicing annual expectations and goals on a daily basis, builds student self-esteem and confidence, while improving attitudes and grades. Enjoy the book and the rewards that come with it.

Exercise 1

Name _____

October

Sun	Mon	Tues	Wed	Thurs	Fri	Sat
			1	2	3	4
5	6	7	8	9	10	11
12	13	14	15	16	17	18
19	20	21	22	23	24	25
26	27	28	29	30	31	

1. Your choir practice is on the first Saturday of the month. The concert is three weeks and one day later. When is the concert? _____

2. You want to buy a new shirt for the concert. It costs $15.93. You make $8.00 a week babysitting. Today is Oct. 11. Do you have time to make enough money to buy the shirt?

   _____

3. You get an allowance of $5.00 every other Saturday. How much allowance will you get during October?

   _____

4. Complete the analogy.

   10 : 30 :: 20 : _____
   a. 23   b. 60   c. 40

5. Insert <, =, or > to make the number sentence true.

   101,000 ⬭ 102,000

6. Finish the number sentence.

   2 + 2 + 2 + 2 = ____ = 2 × 4

7. Complete the pattern.

   67, 69, 71, ____, ____, ____

8. What time will it be 10 minutes after the time shown on the clock?

   ____ : ____

9. 55   55   68   68
    −5   −6   −8   −9
    ___   ___   ___   ___

10. Write the names for these figures.

    _____   _____

Exercise 2

Name _____

1. Amber has 2 nickels and 3 pennies. Michelle has 2 dimes.

   How much money does Amber have?

   _____¢

   How much money does Michelle have?

   _____¢

2. How much more money does Michelle have than Amber?

   Michelle has _____¢ more.

....

3. What time will it be 5 minutes after the time shown on the clock?

   _____:_____

....

4. Complete the analogy.

   5 : 15 :: 55 : _____

   a. 65   b. 75   c. 45

....

5. 2 nickels = ___ dime = _____¢

   4 nickels = ____ dimes = _____¢

   12 nickels = ____ dimes = ____¢

6. Circle the hundreds digits in these numbers.

   432   7,493   1,049

....

7. Shade 4/6 of the doughnuts.

   Insert < or > to show which part is more — the shaded or the unshaded doughnuts.

   $\dfrac{4}{6}$ ⬭ $\dfrac{2}{6}$

....

8. Circle the odd numbers.

   22 23 24 25 99 98 97 96

....

9.
46	28	10
+18	−9	×5

....

10. I am an even number.
    I have 2 digits that are the same.
    I am more than 40 and less than 50.

    What number am I? _____

Exercise 3

Name _____

1. Use this information to complete the graph.

Number of Balls Hit Out of 10 Tries

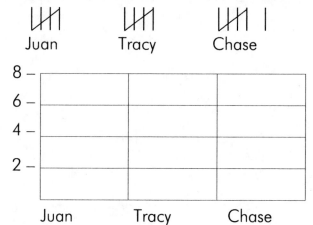

Juan	Tracy	Chase

8 –

6 –

4 –

2 –

| Juan | Tracy | Chase |

2. Who hit the most balls?

_____

3. How many more balls did Chase hit than Juan?

_____

4. What is the fraction of balls that Chase hit?

$$\frac{\quad}{10}$$

5. What time will it be in 15 minutes?

_____:_____

6. Complete the analogies.

7. Put these in order from smallest to largest.

234   369   142   432

_____ _____ _____ _____

8. Label these figures with the correct names.

_____   _____

9.

112	92	12
+231	−8	×2

10. 4 × 7 = ___ + ___ + ___ + ___

4 × 7 = _____

Exercise 4

Name _____

Use the diagram to answer questions 1, 2, and 3.

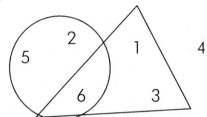

1. What numbers are in the circle but not in the triangle?

_____

2. What numbers are in both the circle and the triangle?

_____

3. What numbers are in neither the circle nor the triangle?

_____

4. It takes 20 minutes to get to school and you have to be there by 8:00 a.m. It is 7:45 a.m. Can you be there on time?

_____

5. Write the numeral for **ten thousand, nine hundred twenty-two**.

_____

6. Write the values on the coins. The total amount equals 75¢.

7. Complete the analogy.

Monday : Tuesday :: Saturday : ____

a. Friday   b. Sunday   c. morning

8.
$$
\begin{array}{ccc}
144 & 136 & 10 \\
+121 & -12 & \times 4 \\
\hline
\end{array}
$$

9. $2 \times 6 =$ ___ $+$ ___ $=$ ____

10. Which color will the spinner below land on most often?

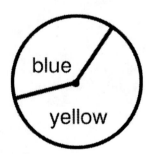

It will land most often on _____.

Why? _____

Exercise 5

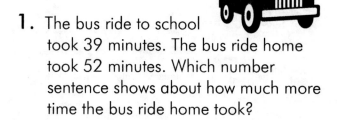

1. The bus ride to school took 39 minutes. The bus ride home took 52 minutes. Which number sentence shows about how much more time the bus ride home took?

   a. 60 – 40 = 20 minutes

   b. 50 – 40 = 10 minutes

2. You need to be at soccer practice by 12:00. What time do you need to leave if it takes 25 minutes to get there?

   _____:_____

3. 1 meter = 100 centimeters

   2 meters = _____ centimeters

   3 meters = _____ centimeters

4. Write a multiplication number sentence for each array.

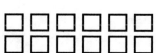 

   ___ x ___ = ___   ___ x ___ = ___

5. How many sides and vertices does this figure have?

   sides _____   vertices _____

6. Are these figures congruent? _____

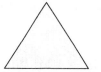

7. Complete the pattern.

   18, 16, 14, ____, ____, ____

   The rule is _____.

8. Circle the tens digit in these numbers.

   422   906   149

   Round each number to the nearest ten.

   _____ _____ _____

9.
25	25	25
x4	x5	x6

10. 18 – 9 = 2 + ___

Exercise 6

1. Maria, Jacob and Michael picked 12 apples. They divided the apples evenly between them. Draw the apples each person received.

Maria   Jacob   Michael

2. Each apple weighed about 8 ounces. About how much did Maria's apples weigh? _____

About how much did all of the apples weigh together?

_____

3. The fifth number is a multiple of ____ and ____.

6 7 8 9 10 11 12

4. Complete the analogy.

 : ♥ :: ☆ :

5. Draw as many lines of symmetry as you can.

6. How much money is shown? _____ ¢

Show a different way of making the same amount of money.

7. Complete the pattern.

65, ____, 75, 80, ____, 90

The rule is _____.

8.
```
  49        66        5
+26       +24      × 6
```

9. 3 × 4 = __ + __ + __ = __

4 × 3 = __ + __ + __ + __

10. Write a number for:

600 + 70 + 5 = _____

500 + 30 + 3 = _____

Exercise 7

Name _____

1. A piano has 36 black keys and 52 white keys. A piano has a bench. How many keys does a piano have?

   A piano has _____ keys.

2. Draw a radius for this circle.

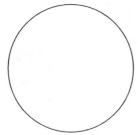

3. Write a multiplication problem for this array.

   ____ × ____ = ____

4. Finish the patten.

   1060, 1059, 1058, _____, _____,

5.
   26   260   10   100
   −18   −180   × 7   × 7
   ___   ____   ___   ___

6. If it takes 20 minutes to wash one car, how long will it take to wash:

   2 cars   3 cars   6 cars
   ____ min.   ____ min.   ____ min.

7. Label each object and tell how many vertices there are.

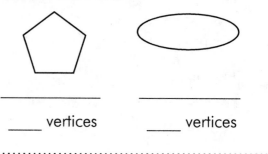

   _____   _____
   ____ vertices   ____ vertices

8. Circle the picture with 3/4 shaded.

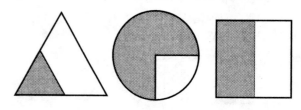

9. Complete the analogy.

10. Insert <, =, or > to make this number sentence true.

   $\frac{1}{2}$ ◯ $\frac{1}{4}$

Exercise 8

Name _____

1. Julie practiced drums everyday. The first day she practiced for 5 minutes. Everyday she practiced 5 minutes more. If she continued with this pattern how many minutes did she practice on the sixth day?

   She practiced for ____ minutes.

2. If her final goal was to practice for 1 hour. How many days would it take to reach her goal? _____

3. If Julie played drums for 40 minutes and she started at 3:10 p.m., what time would she finish?

   ____:____ p.m.

4. Complete the analogy.

   triangle : 3 :: octagon : _____

5. Draw the figure that comes next.

   What is the pattern? _____

   _____

6. Circle the even numbers.

   18   **19**   **20**   **21**   **22**

7. Circle the best estimate for this problem.

problem	estimates		
48	40	40	50
+29	+30	+20	+30

8. Insert <, =, or > to make this a true number sentence.

   696 $\bigcirc$ 600 + 96

9.
180	360	20
+180	−180	× 5

10. Draw lines to divide the circle in thirds. Shade 1/3.

Exercise 9

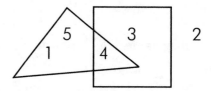

Name _____

1. Jake earned $1.50 for raking leaves. Rebecca earned $1.75 for putting the leaves in the bag. How much more money did Rebecca earn than Jake?

   Rebecca earned _____ more.

2. Jake worked for 30 minutes and Rebecca worked twice as long. How long did Rebecca work? _____

   Who do you think made more money for the time they worked? _____

3. Write in expanded form.

   345 = _____ + _____ + _____

4. Circle the picture that shows 5/6.

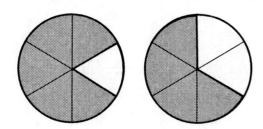

5. Draw all the lines of symmetry.

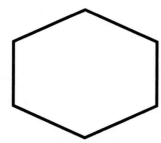

6.

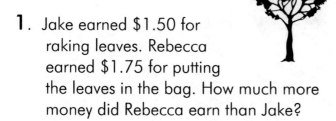

What number is inside the triangle and the square? _____

What number is neither in the square nor triangle? _____

7. Draw a line that is parallel to Main Street.

8.

28	43	8	80
+12	− 6	×3	×3

9. Circle the array that shows 2 × 8.

   a.   b.

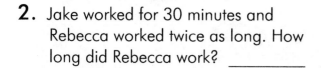

10. If the arrays above were fenced yards, which yard would take the most fence to build? _____

   Which yard would have the most area inside the fence? _____

Exercise 10

1. Abigail collected 172 pennies for the school penny drive. Maria collected 128 pennies. How much money did they collect together?

$ _____

If they collect this amount each day for five days, how much money will they collect?

$_____

2. Complete the number line.

0   .5   1   2   3.0

3. Fill in the chart.

C	5	6	7	8	9
C + 4		10			

4. 4 quarters = $_____

8 quarters = $_____

5. About how long is the watch? ____ units

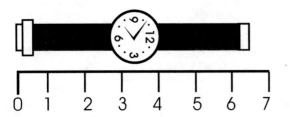

0   1   2   3   4   5   6   7

6. Circle the cone.

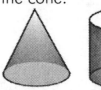

7. Write the numeral for **six thousand nine hundred sixty-three**.

_____

8. Round these numbers to the nearest ten.

98 _____   92 _____

83 _____   89 _____

9.
```
  23          68          68
+           −28         −29
____        ____        ____
  28
```

10. Draw a square. Draw lines to divide the square into 4 equal parts. Shade 2 of the 4 equal parts. Write a fraction for the shaded part.

Exercise 11

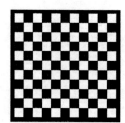

Use this story to answer questions 1, 2 and 3.

Blake played 12 games of checkers. He won 7 games. Elizabeth played 15 games of checkers and won 12 games.

1. How many total games of checkers did Blake and Elizabeth play?

The played _____ games.

How many more games did Elizabeth win than Blake?

Elizabeth won _____ more games.

2. Write a fraction for the games that Blake won and the games he lost.

won _____   lost _____

3. Write a fraction for the games that Elizabeth won and the games she lost.

won _____   lost _____

4. Write a fraction for the part of the butterflies that are circled.

5. Put these in order of least to greatest.

1989   1364   1396

_____   _____   _____

6. Write an addition and a subtraction problem using the numbers 6, 18, 24.

___ − ___ = ___

___ + ___ = ___

7. Circle the tens digit in these numbers and round them to the nearest hundred.

3,392   816   948

_____   _____   _____

8.
```
  13
  23
 +16
```
62
−14

87
−49

9. About how tall is the dog?

a. 3
b. 3½
b. 4

10. $12 \div 2 = 6 \times$ ___

Exercise 12

Use the information on the graph to answer questions 1, 2 and 3.

Books Read in the Read-a-thon

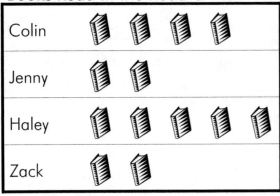

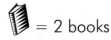 = 2 books

1. How many books did Colin read?

_____ books

2. How many more books did Haley read than Zack?

_____ more books

3. How many books were read by all four children in the Read-a-thon?

_____ books altogether

4. How many faces and vertices does this cube have?

_____ faces

_____ vertices

5. Draw hands on the clock to show the time you will finish your homework if you start at 3:15 and it will take 40 minutes to finish.

6. What is the median of these numbers?

2   3   4   5   6   7   8

The median is _____.

7. Complete the pattern.

41, 43, 45, _____, _____, _____

The rule is _____

8. Insert <, =, or > to make this a true number sentence.

$3\frac{1}{2}$ 3.5

9.
$$
\begin{array}{ccc}
38 & 41 & 13 \\
+44 & -29 & \times 2 \\
\end{array}
$$

10. Draw a line of symmetry.

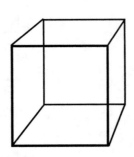

Exercise 13

1. Mike wants to buy a
   baseball. It costs $1.97.
   He already has 89¢ cents.
   How much more does
   Mike need?

   Mike needs $ _____ .

2. How many acute angles does
   this figure have?

   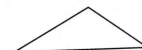

   _____ acute angles

3.
39	22	8
12	16	× 3
+15	+ 44	

4. Complete the drawing to make it
   symmetrical.

5. Complete the analogy.

   234 : 345 :: abc : ____

   a. bcd   **b.** def   **c.** cba

6. Circle the correct name.

   cone

   sphere

   cube

7. Show one way of making $1.31 with
   bills and coins.

8. Insert <, =, or > to make this a true
   number sentence.

   200 ⬯ 189 + 10

9. Complete the pattern.

   196, 197, 198, ____, ____, ____

   The rule is _____ .

10. Circle the best estimate for the sum.

   $2.63
   + 4.29

   about $6.00

   about $7.00

   about $8.00

Exercise 14

Name _____

1. Jan and Steven are both saving to buy a radio. Jan had $2.13 and her mom gave her $1.10 more. Steven has $3.26. Who has more money?

Jan   Steven

How much more money does that person have?

$_____

2. $8 \times 1 = 2 \times$ ____

3. Complete the chart.

fraction	$\frac{1}{10}$	$\frac{3}{10}$		$\frac{9}{10}$
decimal	.1		.7	

4. It took Dave 2 hours to finish reading his book. It took Alden 1 hour and 15 minutes to finish his book. How much longer did it take Dave to read his book?

_____ minutes

5. Circle the expressions that are the same as **20 + 4**.

a. 12×2

b. $(30 - 10) + 5$

c. $36 - 10$

d. $10 + 10 + 4$

6. Draw two congruent figures that each have 3 sides and 3 angles, one of which is a right (90°) angle.

7. Draw one line of symmetry for each of these shapes.

8.

$$\begin{array}{r} 27 \\ -9 \\ \hline \end{array} \qquad \begin{array}{r} 321 \\ +189 \\ \hline \end{array} \qquad \begin{array}{r} 16 \\ \times 2 \\ \hline \end{array}$$

9. Complete the pattern.

142, 132, ____, ____, ____

10. Is the sum of 150 a reasonable estimate for this problem? Why?

$$\begin{array}{r} 96 \\ +51 \\ \hline \end{array}$$

_____

_____

_____

Exercise 15

Number of Home Runs in 10 Games

Sarah					
José					
Gerimo					

 = 2 home runs

1. How many home runs did Sarah and José have in 10 games? _____

2. How many more home runs did José score that Sarah? _____

3. About how many home runs does José score each game? _____

4. So far this season the baseball team has won 10 games and lost 5 games. Which expression would you use to find out how many games they have played altogether?

a. 10 − 5   b. 15 − 10

c. 10 + 5   c. 15 − 5

5. Write the number **one thousand six hundred eighty-seven**.

_____

6.
```
  882        936        12
 +619       −317       × 4
```

7. Are these pentagons congruent?

  _____

8. Round the numbers to the nearest thousand.

2,903   **8,421**   **5,214**

_____   _____   _____

9. Insert <, =, or > to make this a true number sentence.

$1\frac{1}{2}$ ⬭ $1\frac{1}{4}$

10. Draw a line segment two inches long. Label the end points A and B.

Exercise 16

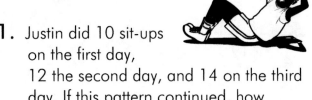

1. Justin did 10 sit-ups on the first day, 12 the second day, and 14 on the third day. If this pattern continued, how many sit-ups did he do on the fifth day?

_____ sit-ups

Use this map for questions 2 and 3. Each intersection is one block.

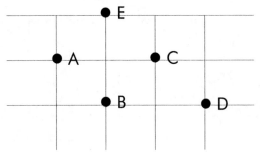

2. Draw the shortest route from point A to point D (stay on the roads). How many blocks is it from A to D?

_____ blocks

3. How many different direct routes can you take from point D to point E? ____

4. Use a ruler to measure side a.

a = ____ inches

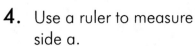

5. About how much is the sum?

$1.39
+ .21

about $1.00
about $1.50
about $1.60

6. Circle the correct name for this shape.

cylinder

cube

7. Draw a right triangle.

8.
```
 28        550       100
 32       −160       × 4
+15
```

9. Write the numeral for:
6 thousands + 8 hundreds + 3 ones

_____

10. Connor is older than Allison but younger than Shannon. Show the three people in order of oldest to youngest.

Exercise 17

Name _____

1. Jill has 4 nickels and 1 quarter. Sarah has 3 dimes and 1 quarter. How much money does each girl have?

   Jill _____   Sarah _____

2. Who has more money and how much more does she have?

   _____ has _____¢ more.

3. Which two shapes are congruent?

   a.   b.   c.

   This shape is a _____?

   a. hexagon
   b. pentagon
   c. octagon

4. Continue the pattern.

   8, 12, 16, ____, ____, ____, ____

   The rule is _____.

5. 2 × 4 = 4 + ___

6.
300	301	302
× 2	× 2	× 2

7. Write the fraction for the shaded part of each picture.

   _____   _____

8.
63	64	65
+9	+9	+9

9. In a bag there are 28 brown, 20 red, 15 yellow, and 12 blue jelly beans. If you reached in without looking, what color would you be **least** likely to pull out?

   _____

10. Write fractions for the different colors of jelly beans in the bag.

    blue $\dfrac{}{75}$ yellow $\dfrac{}{75}$

    red $\dfrac{}{75}$ brown $\dfrac{}{75}$

Exercise 18

Name _____

1. Lisa collected 9 eggs from the hen house. Then she collected 6 more eggs from the yard. How many eggs did Lisa collect altogether? _____

   Draw a picture of how she could divide them into three equal piles.

2. Circle a fraction that represents the shaded part of this drawing.

   ½   ²⁄₈   ⅙

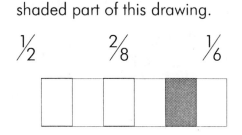

3. $6 \times 2 = 3 \times$ _____

4. Circle the best estimate for the difference.

   $$\begin{array}{r} 1.65 \\ -.12 \\ \hline \end{array}$$

   about 1.50
   about 1.40
   about 1.30

5. Write the numeral for **one hundred forty-four thousand and ninety-three**.

   _____

6.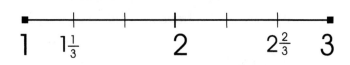

   $$\begin{array}{r} 16 \\ +68 \\ \hline \end{array} \qquad \begin{array}{r} 37 \\ -29 \\ \hline \end{array} \qquad \begin{array}{r} 14 \\ \times 10 \\ \hline \end{array}$$

7. Complete the number line.

   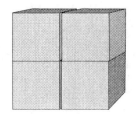

   1    $1\frac{1}{3}$ 2 $2\frac{2}{3}$ 3

8. What is the volume of this solid figure.

   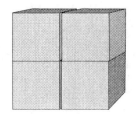

   _____

9. Draw a picture and write a division number sentence to show 16 flowers divided equally into 4 sets.

   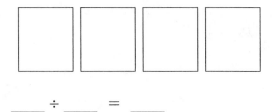

   _____ ÷ _____ = _____

10. Nathan makes $54.00 per week delivering newspapers. What would be a reasonable estimate of what he makes in a month?

    a. $200   b. $250   c. $2,500

Exercise 19

Favorite Lunch Foods

each drawing = 5 people

Name _____

1. What is the least favorite food?

_____

2. How many students like hamburgers?

_____

3. How many more students like pizza than sandwiches?

_____

....

4. These coins total 96¢. Write the value of each coin.

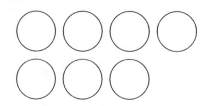

....

5. $5 \times 2 = 20 \div$ ____

6. $12 \div 4 =$

$$\begin{array}{r} 44 \\ -16 \\ \hline \end{array} \qquad \begin{array}{r} 16 \\ \times 10 \\ \hline \end{array}$$

....

7. Finish the pattern.

120, 140, 160, _____, _____

....

8. Each cube has a volume of 8 cubic inches. What is the volume of all of these cubes together?

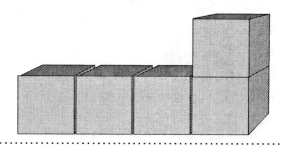

....

9. Insert <, =, or > to make this a true number sentence.

$1\frac{3}{4}$ ◯ $1\frac{1}{4}$

....

10. Complete the comparison.

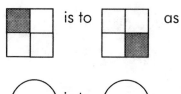

Exercise 20

Name _____

1. Randy has 30 striped pencils. His mom gave him 70 yellow pencils. How many pencils does Randy have now?

_____ pencils

2. If Randy pulls one of the pencils out of the bag without looking, what is the chance that he will pull out a striped pencil?

_____ out of _____

3. Complete the analogy.

70 : 80 :: 102 :: _____

a. 112   **b.** 120   **c.** 92

3. Write a mixed number for this drawing.

_____

4. Circle the odd numbers.

7   12   13   17   18

5. Write the numeral for **two hundred fifty thousand six hundred and fifty-one.**

_____

6. Complete this pattern.

110, 140, 170, _____, _____

7. Divide the crayons into 5 equal groups and write a number sentence.

_____ ÷ _____ = _____

8. Round these numbers to the nearest ten.

65 _____   73 _____

165 _____   1,173 _____

9. It is 7:00 p.m. and you have to be at the concert in half an hour. It takes 5 minutes to get there.

What is the latest time you can leave the house and still be on time?

_____:_____ p.m.

10. What will the temperature be if it drops 20°?

_____ °

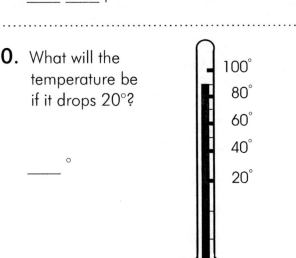

Exercise 21

Name _____

1. Monica has 28 pairs of sunglasses. Two are yellow and the rest are blue. She gave her friend Michelle half of her sunglasses. How many sunglasses does each girl have?

_____ sunglasses each

....

2. Circle the ten thousands place in this number.

148,201

....

3. What time would it have been 25 minutes before the time shown on the clock?

_____:_____

....

4. Write the fraction for each object.

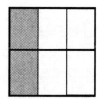   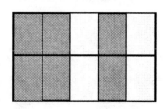

_____   _____

....

5. $2 \times 2 = 8 \div$ _____

$5 \times 3 =$ _____ + _____

6. Write the fact family for 2, 3, and 6

_____ × 2 = 6

2 × _____ = _____

6 ÷ _____ = _____

6 ÷ _____ = _____

....

7. Complete the chart.

x	16	10	22	50
x ÷2	8			

....

8. Put these numbers in order from least to greatest.

122   102   110   150

_____ _____ _____ _____

....

9.
```
  16
  22
 +31
```
```
 1046
 − 28
 ____
```
```
   8
 ×11
```

....

10. Write each decimal as a fraction.

$.4 = \dfrac{}{10}$ $.8 = \dfrac{}{}$

$.34 = \dfrac{}{100}$ $.25 = \dfrac{}{}$

Exercise 22

Name _____

1. What unit of measurement would you use to measure the length of a car?

centimeter   meter   kilometer

....

2. Ian weighs 100 pounds. Tracy weighs less than Ian but more than Marcus. Kelly weighs the least of all and she weighs 97 pounds. What are the possible weights of Tracy and Marcus if they do not weight the same?

Tracy _____   Marcus _____

....

3. 10 : 5 :: 12 : ____

a. 5   **b.** 6   **c.** 7

....

4. Show one way of making $1.85.

....

5. Complete the number sentences for the number family 5, 9 and 45.

$5 \times$ ___ $= 45$

___ $\times$ ___ $=$ ___

___ $\div$ ___ $= 5$

___ $\div$ ___ $=$ ___

6. Circle the best estimate of this product.

$\begin{array}{r} 39 \\ \times 10 \end{array}$ about **300**   **400**   **4000**

....

7. $\begin{array}{r} 12 \\ \times 2 \\ \hline \end{array}$ $\begin{array}{r} 35 \\ -28 \\ \hline \end{array}$ $2\overline{)20}$

....

8. 1 quart = 4 cups

3 quarts = ____ cups

$\dfrac{1}{2}$ quart = ____ cups

....

9. Round these numbers to the nearest hundred.

984 _____   8,842 _____ 1,621 _____

....

10. Write fractions for the shaded and unshaded parts.

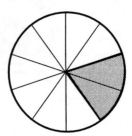

shaded $= \dfrac{}{10}$ unshaded $= \dfrac{}{10}$

Exercise 23

1. Crystal is packing her dolls in boxes. She has 39 dolls. Each box will hold 10 dolls. How many boxes will she need? Draw a picture.

_____ boxes

2. What time will it be in one hour from the time shown on the clock?

____:____

3. Complete the analogy.

47 : 470 :: 93 : ____

a. 930　　**b.** 390　　**c.** 934

4. Which expression is the same as 8 × 4?

a. 35 – 3　　　b. 20 + 11

c. 3 × 12　　　d. 7 × 5

5. Finish the pattern.

296, 297, 299, 302, 306, 311,

_____, _____, _____

6. Complete the fact family.

7 × 8 = ___

8 × ___ = 56

___ ÷ ___ = ___

___ ÷ ___ = ___

7.

44	119	25
+56	−46	×8

8. Circle the best estimate for this product.

$\begin{array}{r} 62 \\ \times\ 3 \\ \hline \end{array}$　about **170　180　200**

9. Circle the tens digit in each number.

21　258　201　5,024

10. Megan wants to buy two books. They cost $4.95 and $6.95. Does she have enough money to buy both books?

What information do you need to solve this problem?

_____

_____

Exercise 24

Name _____

1. Samuel leaves at 11:30 a.m. to go to his grandmother's house. It takes two hours and five minutes to get there. What time will it be when he gets there?

   It will be _____.

2. Divide these apples into four equal groups and write a number sentence that shows the grouping.

   ____ ÷ ____ = ____

3. Write an equivalent expression.

   $26 \div 2 =$ ____ ◯ ____

4. Adam has three coins. Each coin is greater than a penny and less than 50 cents. Show three of the possible combinations of three coins Adam could have.

   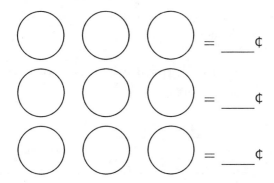

5. $8 \times 6 = 12 \times$ ___

6. Underline the hundreds digit and circle the tens digit in these numbers.

   721   684   6884

7. Round each number above to the nearest hundred.

   _____   _____   _____

8. Write the fraction for the black part of each picture. Circle the picture that shows the largest fraction.

   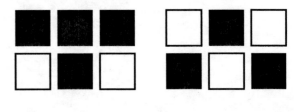

   _____   _____

9.
30	90	18
44	−18	× 6
+24		

10. Each day Joaquin trains for a triathlon by running 3 miles and riding his bike 5 miles. If he does this five days a week, how far does he run and ride during the week?

    ____ miles

Exercise 25

1. Jerome had 46 football cards and 20 baseball cards. He gave 8 football cards to Samantha. How many football cards does he have now?

____ football cards

2. The movie starts at 3:10 and lasts two hours. Draw hands on the clock to show the time the movie will be over.

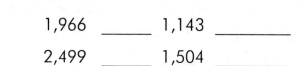

3. $2 \times 10 = 20 \times$ ____

4. Write three letters of the alphabet that are symmetrical and draw the line of symmetry.

_____ _____ _____

5. Draw two parallelograms that are not congruent.

6. Round these numbers to the nearest thousand.

1,966 ____ 1,143 _____

2,499 ____ 1,504 _____

7. Write the missing fractions on the number line.

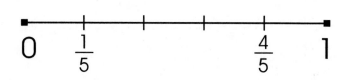

8. Divide this octagon into 8 equal pieces. Shade 1 piece. Write a fraction for the <u>unshaded</u> pieces.

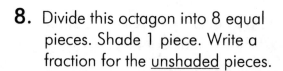

9.

$$\begin{array}{r} 2,000 \\ -\ 499 \\ \hline \end{array} \qquad 8\overline{)32} \qquad \begin{array}{r} 12 \\ \times 10 \\ \hline \end{array}$$

10. Complete the pattern.

128, 148, 168, ____, ____, ____

The rule is _____.

1. It took Monica 32 seconds to run the length of her sidewalk. The next time it took her 13 seconds less. How long did it take her the second time?

It took her ____ seconds.

2. Max is 4 feet tall. David is 16 inches taller than Max. How tall is David?

____ feet ____ inches

3. Dora is taller than Matt but shorter than Joey. Lilly is the shortest. Write their names in order from shortest to tallest.

_____
_____
_____
_____

4. Draw lines to divide this circle into 4 equal parts. Shade ¾ of the circle.

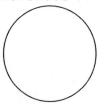

5. Complete the pattern.

2.00, 2.30, 2.60, _____, _____

The rule is _____.

6. $9 + 3 = 3 \times$ ____

7. Round these numbers to the nearest thousand.

9,144 _____

3,499 _____

2,122_____

8. Put these numbers in order from least to greatest.

301, 302, 298, 299

_____ _____ _____ _____

9.
```
 100      41
 -67      39      5)105
 ___     +11
         ___
```

10. Dario has 3 coins in his pocket. The total of the coins is 52¢. What coins could he have?

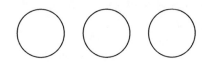

Exercise 27

Number of Newspapers Sold

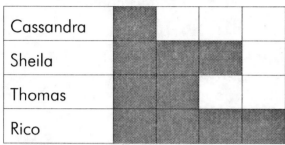

Cassandra				
Sheila				
Thomas				
Rico				

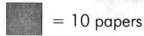 = 10 papers

1. How many newspapers were sold altogether?

_____

2. How many more newspapers did Rico sell than Thomas?

_____ more papers

3. With bills and coins, show one way of making $6.75.

4. Complete the analogy.

A1 : B2 :: F6 : _____

5. It takes Kevin 15 minutes to walk home. What time will Kevin have to leave if he has to be home by 8:30?

____:____

6. Julie's house is at (2, 3). Ben's house is at (4, 3). Label Julie's house and Ben's house.

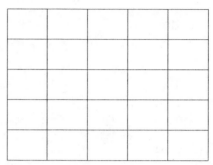

0, 0

7.
$$\begin{array}{r} 173 \\ -28 \\ \hline \end{array}$$
$44 \div 4 =$ ___

8. If the sides of this square are each 2 units long, what is the perimeter?

_____ units

9. Complete the pattern.

$\dfrac{1}{10}$, $\dfrac{3}{10}$, $\dfrac{5}{10}$, ___, ___, ___

10. Write the products. What pattern do you see?

$9 \times 2 =$ ___ $9 \times 5 =$ ___

$9 \times 3 =$ ___ $9 \times 6 =$ ___

$9 \times 4 =$ ___ $9 \times 7 =$ ___

Exercise 28

Name _____

This chart shows how many hot dogs were sold at the fair each day.

day	hot dogs sold
Monday	30
Tuesday	87
Wednesday	99
Thursday	120

1. About how many hot dogs were sold on Tuesday, Wednesday and Thursday?

a. 200   b. 300   c. 400

2. Which day was the busiest?

_____

3. If you were in charge of buying hot dogs for Friday, how many hot dogs would you buy?

a. 150   b. 50   c. 100

4. Stacy watched a show that began an hour and half before the time shown on the clock. What time did the show start?

____:____

5. Circle the correct name.

pyramid   rectangular prism

6. Fill in operation symbols to make this a true number sentence.

81 ◯ 10 ◯ 6 ◯ 77

7. $5 \times 3 = 20 -$ ____

8. Shade the thermometer to show 76°.

```
80   70   60   50   40
```

9.
```
  121        81
 −12         24        3)609
            +16
```

10. Mike has three coins in his pocket. Each coin is less than a quarter. Show four possible combinations of coins that he could have.

_____   _____

_____   _____

Exercise 29

Name _____

1. Jessica walks her dog for 30 minutes. If she starts at 11:04 a.m., what time will she finish walking the dog?

_____ : _____

....

2. How is this trapezoid like a rectangle?

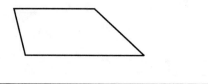

_____

....

3. These coins make 87¢. Write the value of each coin.

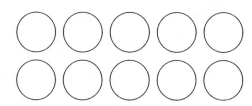

....

4. If you give a clerk $20.00 for a $13.45 purchase, how much change would you get?

_____

....

5. Draw 2 parallel lines. Draw a diagonal line that intersects both of the parallel lines.

6. Round these numbers to the nearest thousand.

4,881 _____   6,645 _____

2,123 _____   10,068 _____

....

7. Complete the pattern.

3 ½, 4, 4 ½, _____, _____, _____

The rule is _____.

....

8. Complete the analogy.

8 : 64 :: 5 : _____

....

9.
149   163
× 3   −58   36 ÷ 6 _____

....

10. Draw a rectangle. Divide the rectangle into 12 equal pieces. Shade 5 of the pieces. Write a fraction for the <u>unshaded</u> pieces.

Exercise 30

Name _____

1. James made 1 goal for his soccer team in the first game, 4 goals in the second game, and 4 goals in the third game. How many goals has James made in the three games? _____

   How many goals did he average per game? _____

2. It is 9:00 a.m. and you have music and math before lunch. Lunch is at 11:30 a.m. If music and math are the same amount of time, how long is music?

   Music is _____ hour _____ minutes.

3. Complete the pattern.

   .25, .50, .75, _____, _____, _____

4. The coins below total $1.51. Write the value of each coin.

   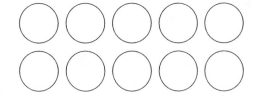

5. Find the perimeter and area of each object.

   ```
   ┌──────────┐        ┌────────┐
   │    5     │ 3      │   4    │ 2
   └──────────┘        └────────┘
   ```

   P = ___   P = ___
   A = ___   A = ___

6. Insert <, =, or > to make this a true number sentence.

   98 ◯ 99 – 3

7. Draw a picture to show 24 ÷ 3.

8. Draw a ray that begins at point A.

   A •

9.
   $$365 \atop +154$$ $$885 \atop -416$$ $6\overline{)88}$

10.
   $$.50 \atop \times\,2$$ $$1.00 \atop \times\,2$$ $$1.50 \atop \times\,2$$

© 2005 Prufrock Press Inc   Math Warm-Ups Grade 3

Exercise 31

1. Tim, Sam, and Amy bring 16 cupcakes each to share with their class. If there are 24 people in the class, how many will each person get?

_____ cupcakes

2. Fill in the missing decimals on the number line.

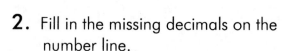

2   2.5

3. Evan earns $7.25 for every dog he takes on a walk. If he walks five dogs a day, how much will he earn per day?

4. Put these numbers in order of least to greatest.

1,846   1,686   1,943   1,523

_____ _____ _____ _____

5. Insert **<**, **=**, or **>** to make this a true number sentence.

646 ⬭ 664 − 20

6. Draw a line that is perpendicular to the line below.

_____

7. Match each figure with its name.

line   a.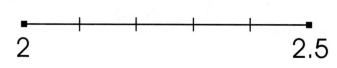

line segment   b.

ray   c.

8. 18 − 9 = 3 × ___

9.   128   95   3)69‾
       +128   −89

10. This is 1/3 of the flags. How many total flags are there?

_____ flags in all

Exercise 32

Name _____

Weights of Dogs

bull dog						
Labrador						
poodle						
basset hound						

 = 10 pounds

1. How much does the heaviest dog weight?

_____

2. How much does the basset hound weigh?

_____

3. How much more does the Labrador weight than the poodle?

_____

....

4. Which is not a regular polygon?

a. [ ]   b. ◇   c. ⬠

....

5. Complete the analogy.

2 cups : pint :: 2 pints : ____

a. gallon   b. quart   c. liter

6. Write the fraction for the <u>shaded</u> part of each picture below. Circle the largest fraction.

_____   _____

....

7. How much money is $\frac{1}{10}$ of a dollar?

_____ ¢

....

8. $5 \times 3 = 30 \div$ ____

....

9.
$$\begin{array}{r} 17 \\ 83 \\ +16 \\ \hline \end{array}$$
$$\begin{array}{r} 10,144 \\ -9,838 \\ \hline \end{array}$$
$$64 \div 8 = \_\_\_$$

....

10. Julia's house is the same distance from Mary's house as from Janet's house.
How many miles is it for Mary to walk to Janet's house?   _____ miles

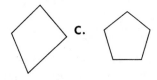

↑ Janet   ↑ Julia   ↑ Mary

Exercise 15

Number of Home Runs in 10 Games

Sarah					
José					
Gerimo					

 = 2 home runs

1. How many home runs did Sarah and José have in 10 games? _____

2. How many more home runs did José score that Sarah? _____

3. About how many home runs does José score each game? _____

4. So far this season the baseball team has won 10 games and lost 5 games. Which expression would you use to find out how many games they have played altogether?

   a. 10 – 5   b. 15 – 10
   c. 10 + 5   c. 15 – 5

5. Write the number **one thousand six hundred eighty-seven**.

   _____

6.
   882   936   12
   +619   −317   × 4

7. Are these pentagons congruent?

  _____

8. Round the numbers to the nearest thousand.

   2,903   8,421   5,214

   _____   _____   _____

9. Insert <, =, or > to make this a true number sentence.

   $1\frac{1}{2}$ ◯ $1\frac{1}{4}$

10. Draw a line segment two inches long. Label the end points A and B.

Exercise 16

Name _____

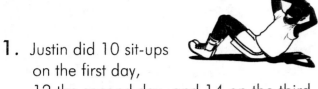

1. Justin did 10 sit-ups on the first day, 12 the second day, and 14 on the third day. If this pattern continued, how many sit-ups did he do on the fifth day?

_____ sit-ups

Use this map for questions 2 and 3. Each intersection is one block.

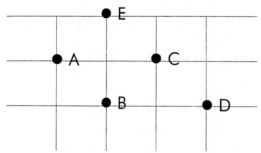

2. Draw the shortest route from point A to point D (stay on the roads). How many blocks is it from A to D?

_____ blocks

3. How many different direct routes can you take from point D to point E? _____

4. Use a ruler to measure side a.

a = _____ inches

5. About how much is the sum?

$1.39
+ .21

about $1.00
about $1.50
about $1.60

6. Circle the correct name for this shape.

cylinder

cube

7. Draw a right triangle.

8.
```
 28        550       100
 32       -160       × 4
+15       ____       ___
___
```

9. Write the numeral for:
6 thousands + 8 hundreds + 3 ones

_____

10. Connor is older than Allison but younger than Shannon. Show the three people in order of oldest to youngest.

Exercise 17

Name _____

1. Jill has 4 nickels and 1 quarter. Sarah has 3 dimes and 1 quarter. How much money does each girl have?

   Jill _____   Sarah _____

2. Who has more money and how much more does she have?

   _____ has _____¢ more.

3. Which two shapes are congruent?

   a.   b. 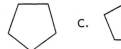   c.

   This shape is a _____?

   a. hexagon
   b. pentagon
   c. octagon

4. Continue the pattern.

   8, 12, 16, ____, ____, ____, ____

   The rule is _____.

5. $2 \times 4 = 4 + $ ___

6. $\begin{array}{r} 300 \\ \times\ 2 \\ \hline \end{array}$ $\begin{array}{r} 301 \\ \times\ 2 \\ \hline \end{array}$ $\begin{array}{r} 302 \\ \times\ 2 \\ \hline \end{array}$

7. Write the fraction for the shaded part of each picture.

   _____   _____

8. $\begin{array}{r} 63 \\ +9 \\ \hline \end{array}$ $\begin{array}{r} 64 \\ +9 \\ \hline \end{array}$ $\begin{array}{r} 65 \\ +9 \\ \hline \end{array}$

9. In a bag there are 28 brown, 20 red, 15 yellow, and 12 blue jelly beans. If you reached in without looking, what color would you be **least** likely to pull out?

   _____

10. Write fractions for the different colors of jelly beans in the bag.

   blue $\dfrac{\ \ }{75}$ yellow $\dfrac{\ \ }{75}$

   red $\dfrac{\ \ }{75}$ brown $\dfrac{\ \ }{75}$

Exercise 18

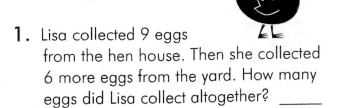

1. Lisa collected 9 eggs from the hen house. Then she collected 6 more eggs from the yard. How many eggs did Lisa collect altogether? _____

   Draw a picture of how she could divide them into three equal piles.

2. Circle a fraction that represents the shaded part of this drawing.

   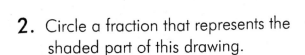

   $\frac{1}{2}$ $\frac{2}{8}$ $\frac{1}{6}$

   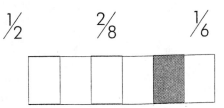

3. $6 \times 2 = 3 \times$ ____

4. Circle the best estimate for the difference.

   $\begin{array}{r} 1.65 \\ -.12 \\ \hline \end{array}$ about 1.50

   about 1.40

   about 1.30

5. Write the numeral for **one hundred forty-four thousand and ninety-three**.

   _____

6. $\begin{array}{r} 16 \\ +68 \\ \hline \end{array}$ $\begin{array}{r} 37 \\ -29 \\ \hline \end{array}$ $\begin{array}{r} 14 \\ \times 10 \\ \hline \end{array}$

7. Complete the number line.

   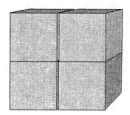

   1    $1\frac{1}{3}$ 2 $2\frac{2}{3}$ 3

8. What is the volume of this solid figure.

   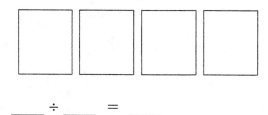

   _____

9. Draw a picture and write a division number sentence to show 16 flowers divided equally into 4 sets.

   ____ ÷ ____ = ____

10. Nathan makes $54.00 per week delivering newspapers. What would be a reasonable estimate of what he makes in a month?

    a. $200   b. $250   c. $2,500

© 2005 Prufrock Press Inc   Math Warm-Ups Grade 3

Exercise 19

Name _____

Favorite Lunch Foods

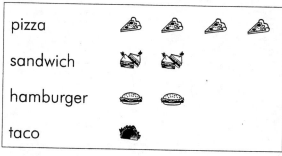

each drawing = 5 people

1. What is the least favorite food?

_____

2. How many students like hamburgers?

_____

3. How many more students like pizza than sandwiches?

_____

4. These coins total 96¢. Write the value of each coin.

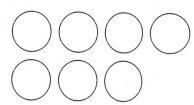

5. $5 \times 2 = 20 \div$ ____

6. $12 \div 4 =$

$$\begin{array}{cc} 44 & 16 \\ -16 & \times 10 \end{array}$$

7. Finish the pattern.

120, 140, 160, _____, _____

8. Each cube has a volume of 8 cubic inches. What is the volume of all of these cubes together?

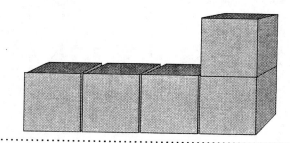

9. Insert <, =, or > to make this a true number sentence.

$$1\frac{3}{4} \bigcirc 1\frac{1}{4}$$

10. Complete the comparison.

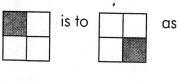

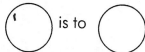

Exercise 33

1. Kate, John and Jerry each have 25 tennis balls. How many tennis balls do they all have together?

____ balls

Two friends join them to play tennis. They share all the balls equally. How many balls does each person have?

_____ balls each

2. The time of the tennis match is shown on the clock. If it is 11:30 now, do they have enough time to practice for half an hour and have a snack?

_____

3. Complete the analogy.

25 : 5 :: 49 : ____

4. Finish the fact family.

$3 \times 7 =$ ____

____ $\times$ ____ = ____

____ $\div$ ____ = ____

____ $\div$ ____ = ____

5. How long is this pen? ____ units

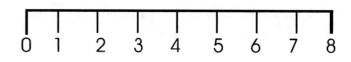

6. $20 \times 7 = 10 \times$ ____

7. 1 kilogram = 1000 grams

2 kilograms = _____ grams

$2 \frac{1}{2}$ kilograms = _____ grams

3 kilograms = _____ grams

8. Insert **<**, **=**, or **>** to make this a true number sentence.

$7 \times 11 \bigcirc 6 \times 13$

9.
$$\begin{array}{r} 160 \\ \times\ 2 \\ \hline \end{array} \qquad \begin{array}{r} 16 \\ \times 20 \\ \hline \end{array} \qquad 32 \div 2 = \ \underline{\ \ }$$

10. If Janet rides her bike from her house to Mary's and then back home, how many miles will she travel?

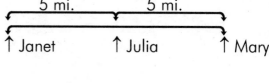

____ miles

Exercise 34

1. At the meeting of the Creepy Crawly Insect Club Elizabeth brought 16 bugs, Ann brought 24 bugs, and Jake brought 8 bugs. How many more bugs did Elizabeth bring than Jake?

_____ more bugs

2. The Insect Club makes 10¢ for each bug they take to the zoo. How much money could they make from this meeting?

$_____

3. Complete the analogy.

16 : 32 :: 9 : _____

a. 18   **b.** 17   **c.** 81

4. Draw and label the diameter and radius of this circle.

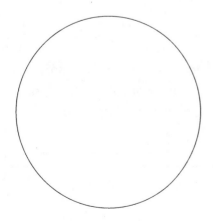

5. What would be a reasonable estimate for the product?

$$\begin{array}{r} 63 \\ \times 29 \\ \hline \end{array}$$ about 170   1800   2000

6. Circle $\frac{4}{8}$ the cupcakes.

7. If these cupcakes are going to be shared among 9 people, are there enough for each person to have 2 cupcakes each? _____

Will there be any left over? _____

8. $2 \times 10 = 10 +$ ___

9. $\begin{array}{r} \$1.36 \\ \times\ \ \ 4 \\ \hline \end{array}$ $\begin{array}{r} \$5.98 \\ -2.96 \\ \hline \end{array}$ $7\overline{)\$49.35}$

10. Ellie is taller than Betsy but shorter than Maggie. Out of these three children, who is the second tallest?

_____

Exercise 35

Name _____

Use this information to complete questions
1, 2, 3, and 4.

name	races won
Juan	IIII
Travis	IIII I
Miguel	IIII
Brent	III

1. Make a graph to represent the same
information in the table above.

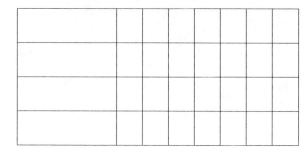

2. How many more races did Travis win
than Miguel?

_____

3. If Juan and Miguel were on one team
and their scores combined, would they
beat the combined scores of a team
with Travis and Brent on it?

_____

4. A runner gets 10 points for each race
he wins, and 100 points are needed to
to go the semi-finals. How many more
points does Travis need?

_____ points

5. For each multiplication problem, write
a related division problem.

$5 \times 9 = 45$ $45 \div$ ___ = ___

$6 \times 12 = 72$ ___ $\div$ ___ = ___

$7 \times 15 = 105$ ___ $\div$ ___ = ___

6. Shade 3/7 of the blimps.

7. $\dfrac{1}{4} + \dfrac{2}{4} =$ $\dfrac{3}{4} - \dfrac{2}{4} =$

$\dfrac{4}{8} + \dfrac{2}{8} =$ $\dfrac{5}{8} - \dfrac{3}{8} =$

8. $3 \times 4 = 144 \div$ ___

9.
$$\begin{array}{r} 10{,}097 \\ -\ 8{,}838 \\ \hline \end{array}$$
$2\overline{)37}$
$$\begin{array}{r} 1118 \\ \times\ \ \ 3 \\ \hline \end{array}$$

10. Underline the ten thousands place in
the numbers below.

289,456   89,456   19,456

Exercise 36

Name _____

1. Joey brought 7 toy cars to school. Sarah brought 3 cars and Max brought 10 cars. If they divided the toys into 4 equal groups, how many would be in each group?

____ in each group

2. The number **2,376** has:

___ thousands + ___ hundreds +

___ tens + ___ ones

3. Write the names of these geometric shapes.

_____   _____

Money Collected for the Field Trip

week 1	week 2	week 3	week 4
$25.00	$45.00	$70.00	$35.00

4. How much money has been collected so far? $_____.

5. There are 25 children in the class. It costs $10.00 per child for the field trip. How much more money has to be collected? $_____.

6. Put these in order from least to greatest.

1.25   .75   1.5   1.75

_____

7. Complete the chart.

days worked	1	2	3	5
money earned	$35			

8. $7 \times 6 = 3 \times 2 \times$ ____

9. $\begin{array}{r} \$4.44 \\ -3.45 \\ \hline \end{array}$ $2\overline{)\$4.44}$ $\begin{array}{r} \$.44 \\ \times\ 3 \\ \hline \end{array}$

10. Circle the hundreds place in the numbers. Then round each number to the nearest thousand.

2,453   2,553

_____   _____

Exercise 37

Name _____

1. Tom has 16 paper airplanes. Mary has 4 airplanes less than Tom, and Chad has 1 more than Tom. How many airplanes do they have altogether?

_____   _____   _____
Tom   Mary   Chad

_____ airplanes in all

2. How could they divide the airplanes so they each got an equal amount?

_____ airplanes each

3. Morgan started swimming at 2:30 p.m. He swam laps for 20 minutes and practiced diving for 35 minutes. When did he get out of the pool?

_____ : _____

4. Continue the pattern.

44, 48, 52, _____, _____, _____

5. Fill in the missing numbers in this chart.

×	11	12	13	14
3		36		
4				56
5	55			

6. Shade the squares to make the number sentence true.

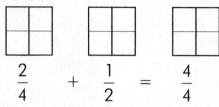

$\frac{2}{4}$ + $\frac{1}{2}$ = $\frac{4}{4}$

7. Round each number to the nearest ten cents.

$1.48 _____ $8.20 _____

$1.13 _____ $1.29 _____

8. Show a way of making $1.11 with four coins.

◯ ◯ ◯ ◯

9.

22
43
+62

15
× 4

3)126

10. Janet has 3 coins in her pocket. They are each less than a quarter. One is a nickel. What are four possible combinations of coins she could have?

N, _____, _____   N, _____, _____

N, _____, _____   N, _____, _____

Exercise 38

February

Sun	Mon	Tues	Wed	Thurs	Fri	Sat
				1	2	3
4	5	6	7	8	9	10
11	12	13	14	15	16	17
18	19	20	21	22	23	24
25	26	27	28			

1. Max has a spelling test every Friday. How many spelling tests will he have this month?

    ____

2. Carrie has a birthday on the third Tuesday in February. What will the date of her birthday be?

    Her birthday will be February ____.

3. Carrie needs to send out invitations to her party 12 days before her birthday. On what date should she mail the invitations?

    _____, February ____

4. Complete the analogy.

    uni : one :: tri : _____

5. The coins below total $2.00. Write the value of each coin.

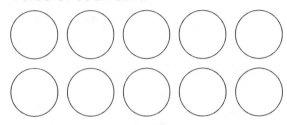

6. Insert <, =, or > to make this a true number sentence.

    8 × 9 ◯ 71

7. Write the names of each geometric object.

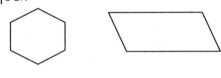

    _____   _____

8. (2 × 3) × 4 = 2 × (__ × __) = ___

9. 1044   22   66 ÷ 2 = ___
    −832   ×11
    _____   _____

10. Round the numbers to the nearest thousand.

    6,450 _____   1,569 _____

    6,621 _____   2,386 _____

Exercise 39

The following chart shows the results of surveying 20 girls and 20 boys on their preference for canvas or leather tennis shoes.

girls		boys	
canvas	leather	canvas	leather
✓✓✓	✓✓	✓✓	✓
✓✓	✓✓✓		✓✓
✓	✓✓✓✓	✓✓	✓✓✓
	✓✓	✓✓✓	✓✓
	✓✓✓	✓	✓✓✓✓

1. Make a tally record of the results.

	canvas	leather
girls		
boys		

2. Make a bar graph of the results.

3. What fraction of the total number of people liked leather?

$$\frac{}{40}$$

4. How many flat faces does a cylinder have?

___ flat faces

5. Circle $\frac{2}{10}$ of the cars.

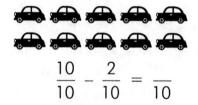

$$\frac{10}{10} - \frac{2}{10} = \frac{}{10}$$

6. If each side of a triangle is 18 cm., what is the perimeter?

_____ cm.

7. Write in expanded form.

845 = _____ + _____ + _____

8. 12 × 8 = 32 × ___

9.
$$\begin{array}{r} 1{,}169 \\ +1{,}241 \\ \hline \end{array} \qquad \begin{array}{r} \$1.84 \\ -\ .25 \\ \hline \end{array} \qquad 6\overline{)420}$$

10. Laurie has 3 packs of gum. Each pack has 15 pieces in it. How many pieces of gum does she have?

____ pieces

Exercise 40

Name _____

1. Cindy and Lori want to buy hamburgers and ice cream. Cindy has $1.53 and Lori has $1.98. If they combine their money, what can they buy?

 = $1.50    = 50¢

____ hamburgers   ____ ice creams

....

2. Hiram takes medicine every 4 hours. If he takes his first dose at 7:00 a.m., when will he take his next three doses?

_____   _____   _____

....

3. Complete the analogy.

30 minutes : $\frac{1}{2}$ :: 45 minutes : ____

....

4. Draw 2 congruent shapes that have at least one right angle.

....

5. About how much would a fork weigh?

3 ounces   3 pounds   30 pounds

6. Draw a picture to show $\frac{3}{6} + \frac{1}{6} = \frac{4}{6}$.

....

7. About how long is this alligator? ____

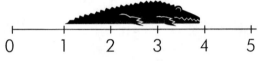

0   1   2   3   4   5

....

8. $7\overline{)665}$ Check by multiplying.

....

9.
$$\begin{array}{ccc} 4 & 60 & 64 \\ \times 4 & \times 4 & \times 4 \\ \hline \end{array}$$

....

10. Round these numbers to the nearest ten and find the sum.

$$\begin{array}{ll} 42 \rightarrow\ 40 & 281 \\ +69 \rightarrow +70 & +963 \\ \hline \end{array}$$

$$\begin{array}{ll} 129 & 304 \\ +810 & +188 \\ \hline \end{array}$$

Exercise 41

Name _____

Use this graph to answer questions 1, 2 and 3.

Favorite Pizza Flavors

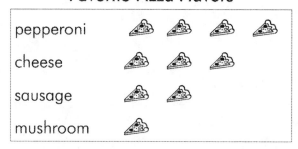

 = 2 people

1. How many people are represented by the graph?

_____ people

2. How many more people like cheese pizza than mushroom pizza?

_____ more people

3. Each pizza is cut into 12 pieces. How many pizzas would you have to order so that each person who voted for pepperoni could have 3 pieces?

_____ pizzas

4. Shade 5/6 of the cats.

5. $\dfrac{3}{9} + \dfrac{2}{9} =$

6. Complete the pattern.

$\dfrac{2}{10}, \dfrac{4}{10}, \dfrac{6}{10}$ ____, ____, ____

The rule is _____.

7. Which shape does not belong?

8. $.6 = \dfrac{}{10}$ $.08 = \dfrac{}{100}$

9. 1/10 of $1.00 = 10¢

2/10 of $1.00 = _____ ¢

7/10 of $1.00 = _____ ¢

10. Amy has more ribbons than Jill or Tasha. Tasha has more than Jill. Danielle has the most ribbons. Show the girls in order of who has the most ribbons to who has the least ribbons.

_____ most

_____

_____

_____ least

Exercise 42

1. Jorge caught 10 fish, Tom caught 2 fish and Raul caught 6 fish. How many fish did they catch together?

_____ fish altogether

If they divided the fish evenly among the three of them, how many fish would each person get?

_____ fish each

2. Mohammad caught 3 fish the first day, 5 fish the second day, 7 fish the third day. If this pattern continues, how many fish will he catch on the seventh day?

day	1	2	3	4	5	6	7
fish	3	5	7				

_____ fish

3. Mohammad doubled the time he spent fishing each day. The first day he spent half an hour. How much time did he spend fishing on the seventh day?

day	1	2	3	4	5	6	7
time	$\frac{1}{2}$	1	2				

_____ hours

4. $609 = $ _____ $\times 3$

5. Write the numeral for **one million two hundred thousand forty**.

_____

6. Round these numbers to the nearest hundred.

63 _____   2,273 _____

1,163 _____   443 _____

7. How much change would you get back from $10.00 if you spent $5.65 on lunch.

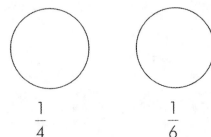

$ _____

8. $12 \times 5 = 3 + $ _____

9. $8 + 6 + 2 = $ _____

$80 + 60 + 20 = $ _____

$\frac{6}{10} - \frac{3}{10} = $ _____

10. Draw lines and shade to show

$\frac{1}{4}$ $\frac{1}{6}$

Exercise 43

1. Bianca wants to buy a camera that costs $51.89. She already has $13.52. How much money does she need before she can buy the camera?

   $_____

2. Circle the best estimate.

   28
   +64   about   80   90   100

3. Complete the analogy.

   78 : 80 :: 46 : ____

   a. 44   b. 48   c. 40

4. How long is this shovel?

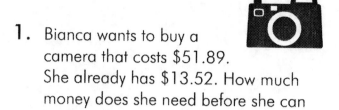

   0   1   2   3   4   5

5. Write a mixed number for the shaded part.

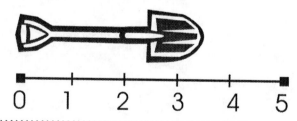

   _____

6. Shade to show 3/8.

   Complete the number sentence.

   $$\frac{3}{8} + \frac{5}{8} = \frac{}{8}$$

7. Insert <, =, or > to make this a true number sentence.

   .75 ◯ .50 + .25

8. 20   100   120
    × 2   × 2   × 2

9. If a recipe calls for 2½ cups of milk, how much milk is needed if you double the recipe?

   ____ cups = ___ pints + ___ cups

10. Jorge, Toby, and Hilda sit in three seats in the front row of the class. What are three different ways the three friends can sit?

   _____   _____

   _____   _____

   _____   _____

Exercise 44

Name _____

1. Sergio jumped on the trampoline each day. The first day he jumped for 4 minutes. He jumped for 8 minutes on the second day and 12 minutes on the third day. If he continued with this pattern how long would he jump on the sixth day?

day	1	2	3	4	5	6
minutes	4	8	12			

_____ minutes

2. At 2 years old, a baby boy is about one half his adult height. If 2-year old Justin is 3 feet 2 inches, about how tall will he be when he reaches his adult height?

_____ feet _____ inches

3. School starts at 8:00 a.m. and ends at 3:00 p.m. How long is the school day?

_____ hours

4. Show one way of making $6.90 with the fewest coins and bills.

5. Count on by tens.

25, _____, _____, _____

6. Put these numbers in order of least to greatest.

$2.04 $2.40 $2.50 $2.55

_____

7. This is 1/2 of the candy. How many pieces are there altogether?

_____ pieces of candy

8. 3 × 5 = _____

30 × 5 = _____

33 × 5 = _____

9. 57 − 7 = _____

57 − 8 = _____

57 − 9 = _____

10. What two months come between January and April?

_____   _____

Exercise 45

Name _____

1. Josh and Haley both got 22 valentines each. Bucky got 23 valentines. How many valentines did Josh, Haley and Bucky get all together?

_____ valentines

....

2. Draw the next two figures.

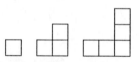

....

3. Andrea has to leave in one hour for piano lessons. What time will she have to leave if it is 2:10 p.m. now?

____:____

....

4. Circle the best estimate for the sum.

$$\begin{array}{r} 780 \\ +230 \\ \hline \end{array}$$ about   800   900   1,000

....

5. Write the name of each object below.

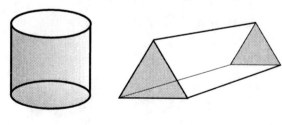

_____   _____

6. Draw lines in the rectangle and shade to show 2/8.

Complete the number sentence.

$$\frac{2}{8} + \frac{\ }{8} = \frac{8}{8}$$

....

7. Draw a shape that has this line as a line of symmetry.

....

8.
$$\begin{array}{r} 166 \\ -144 \\ \hline \end{array}$$ $$\begin{array}{r} 9118 \\ +9918 \\ \hline \end{array}$$ $$\begin{array}{r} 19 \\ \times 5 \\ \hline \end{array}$$

....

9. $6 \times 3 = 2 \times$ ___

....

10. You have 4 white marbles, 2 green marbles, and 5 blue marbles in a bag. You pull three marbles out of the bag without looking. Is it possible to pull out the combination below?

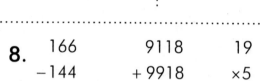

yes   no   Ⓖ   Ⓖ   Ⓖ

yes   no   Ⓦ   Ⓦ   Ⓦ

yes   no   Ⓑ   Ⓑ   Ⓑ

Exercise 46

1. Damien delivers newspapers to 36 different homes each month. He divides the newspapers into 2 equal piles. How many papers are in each pile?

   _____

2. Damien gets $5.00 per month for each home. How much does he earn in one month?

   $_____

   If he has to spend $10.00 for rubber bands each month, how much does he make after expenses?

   $_____

3. Complete the T chart.

	× 2
6	12
10	
12	
20	

4. $7 \times 4 = 2 \times$ ____

5. Find the average of these numbers.

   1, 2, 3, 4, 5, 5, 6, 6

   _____

6. $8 \times 4 =$ ___

   $4 \times$ ___ $=$ ___

   $32 \div$ ___ $=$ ___

   ___ $\div$ ___ $=$ ___

7. $1,000 \times 10 =$ _____

8. The class is giving animal reports. Three reports can be heard in 30 minutes. How long is each report? _____ minutes

   How many reports can be given in one hour? _____ reports

9. $\begin{array}{r} 44 \\ 26 \\ +11 \\ \hline \end{array}$ $\begin{array}{r} 20 \\ \times 5 \\ \hline \end{array}$ $5\overline{)103}$

10. Mandy has three coins in her pocket. One coin is a quarter and one is a penny. List all the combinations of coins that could be in her pocket.

    Q, P, ____   Q, P, ____

    Q, P, ____   Q, P, ____

Exercise 47

Name _____

Favorite Cookies

coconut	$\cancel{||||}$
sugar	$||$
chocolate	$\cancel{||||}\ |$
peanut butter	$|||$
vanilla cream	$||$

1. Use the information to complete the graph.

coconut						
sugar						
chocolate						
peanut butter						
vanilla cream						

$\boxed{}$ = 2 votes

2. How many votes are represented by the graph? _____

3. How many more students like chocolate cookies than peanut butter cookies?

____

4. Is spinner A a fair spinner? _____
Make spinner B unfair.

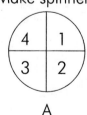 

A   B

5. How many legs will a herd of twelve elephants have?

____ legs

6. Count on by 10's.

613, 623, _____, _____, _____

7. Draw a shape that is congruent to this trapezoid.

8. $6 \times 2 = 2 \times 2 \times \underline{} \times \underline{} \times \underline{} \times \underline{}$

9.
68	182	9110
+41	× 4	− 96

10. What weight would you add to make the scale balance? What side do you need to add the weight to?

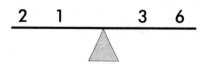

I would add a ___ pound weight to the _____ side.

Exercise 48

Name _____

September

Sun	Mon	Tues	Wed	Thur	Fri	Sat
		1	2	3	4	5
6	7	8	9	10	11	12
13	14	15	16	17	18	19
20	21	22	23	24	25	26
27	28	29	30			

1. Christine's birthday is on the fourth Friday. What is the date of her birthday? _____

2. School starts on Monday of the first full week. How many days will school be in session during the month? _____

3. Derek walks to school on Tuesdays and Thursdays. He buys his lunch on even numbered days. How many days will he walk and buy lunch on the same day?

_____

4. What are the first three prime numbers after the number 2?

_____   _____   _____

5. 720 ÷ 8 = ____

6. I am a two-digit number. My one's digit is an odd number less than 5. My ten's digit is 1 greater than my one's digit. What numbers could I be?

_____   _____

7. How long is the train? _____ cm.

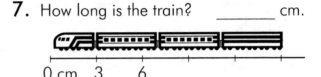

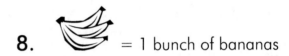

0 cm   3   6

8. 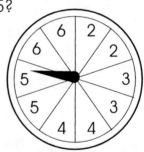 = 1 bunch of bananas

How many bananas will be in five bunches?

____ bananas

9. What is the probability of landing on the number 5?

10.
.25	.25	.25	.25
× 2	× 3	× 4	× 8

Name _____

1. Andy can run the 50-yard dash in 20 seconds. Jay can run it in 18 seconds.

How much longer does it take Andy to run the 50-yard dash than Jay?

_____ seconds

2. About how long do you think it would take Andy to run a 100-yard dash?

_____ seconds

3. Label the points (1,1), (1,4), (5,1) and (5,4).

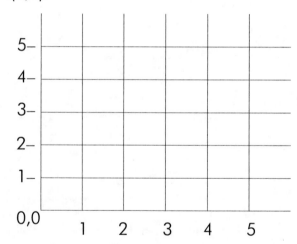

4. Give directions for the shortest route from point (5,4) to point (1,1).

_____

_____

_____

5. Write **5,346** in expanded form.

_____ + _____ + _____ + ___

6. Complete the chart.

×9	27							
		3	4	5	6	7	8	9
×8	24							

7. Write the names for these types of triangles.

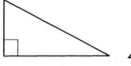 

_____   _____

8. 40   400   4000
      ×2   × 3   × 4

9. Complete the number line.

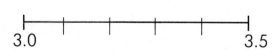
3.0   3.5

10. 4)$58.00 $13.61
                      ×   5

Exercise 50

1. Chase has 30 chopsticks. He wants to share them equally with two of his friends. How many will each person get?

____ chopsticks

....

2. Complete the analogy.

34 : 68 :: 42 : ____

a. 64   **b.** 84   **c.** 74

....

3. If it is 5:10 p.m., and dinner is in 40 minutes. What time is dinner?

____:____

....

4. Show the amount each person will get if you divide $20.50 equally with one other person.

....

5. Put these numbers in order from least to greatest.

10.50   10.05   10.09   10.90

_____

6. Shade one circle to show 3/6. Shade the other circle to show an equal fraction.

$$\frac{3}{6} = \frac{}{8}$$

....

7. Count on by fives.

35.5, 40.5, ____, ____, ____

....

8. $9 \times 2 = 36 \div$ ___

....

9.
$$\begin{array}{ccc} 8{,}248 & 110 & 13 \\ +1{,}899 & -104 & \times 13 \end{array}$$

....

10. Hiro has four pets that he keeps in cages. The sheep's cage is between the snake and the mouse. The turtle is in the first cage and next to the snake. Draw lines between the animals and the locations of their cages.

1st   2nd   3rd   4th

Exercise 51

Name _____

1. Monica picked 16 strawberries, Kristen picked 25, and Michael picked 21. How many strawberries did they pick all together?_____

   If they picked these in a half hour, how many can they pick in 1 hour? _____

2. If they started picking at 6:00 p.m. and picked for an hour and a half, what time would they finish?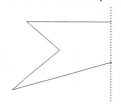

   _____:_____

3. Show 55° on this thermometer.

   80　70　60　50　40

4. Circle 1/4 of the snowflakes.

   ❋ ❋ ❋ ❋ ❋ ❋ ❋ ❋
   ❋ ❋ ❋ ❋ ❋ ❋ ❋ ❋

5. Circle the hexagon.

   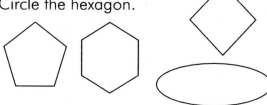

6. Finish the drawing to make a symmetrical shape.

7. What is the area and perimeter of this rectangle?

   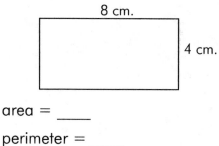
   8 cm.
   4 cm.

   area = _____

   perimeter = _____

8. Which would you use to measure how much water is in a bucket?

   a. meter　　b. gram　　c. liter

9. How many faces, edges, and vertices does this pyramid have?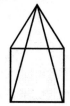

   ___ faces

   ___ edges

   ___ vertices

10.
    60　　　　200　　　　260
    × 5　　　× 5　　　　× 5

Exercise 52

Name _____

1. Use the information to finish the graph.

Favorite Flavors of Ice Cream

lemon	|||
strawberry	|||	
chocolate	||| |||
vanilla	||||

Favorite Flavors of Ice Cream

lemon			
strawberry			
chocolate			
vanilla			
	2	4	6	8

2. If you buy 1 pint of ice cream for each person, how much strawberry ice cream should you buy?

___ pints

3. How much chocolate ice cream should you buy?

___ pints = ___ quarts

4. If a pint of ice cream costs $2.69 and a quart costs $5.29, is it cheaper to buy pints or quarts? _____

5. $3\overline{)123}$ $9\overline{)\$9.45}$

6. Shade 2/5.

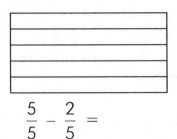

$$\frac{5}{5} - \frac{2}{5} =$$

7. What two things must a square have to be a square?

_____

_____

8. I am greater than 20 and less than 50. My digits are both even numbers. What numbers could I be?

_____

9.
$$\begin{array}{r} 36 \\ +48 \\ \hline \end{array} \qquad \begin{array}{r} 1000 \\ -900 \\ \hline \end{array} \qquad \begin{array}{r} 208 \\ \times\ 2 \\ \hline \end{array}$$

10.
$$\begin{array}{r} 19 \\ \times\ 2 \\ \hline \end{array} \qquad \begin{array}{r} 19 \\ \times\ 3 \\ \hline \end{array} \qquad \begin{array}{r} 19 \\ \times\ 4 \\ \hline \end{array}$$

$$\begin{array}{r} 20 \\ \times 2 \\ \hline \end{array} \qquad \begin{array}{r} 20 \\ \times 3 \\ \hline \end{array} \qquad \begin{array}{r} 20 \\ \times 4 \\ \hline \end{array}$$

Exercise 53

1. Use the information to finish the graph.

Carnival Hats

José |
Roxanne |
Edwardo |
Shiran |

Carnival Hats

José						
Roxanne						
Edwardo						
Shiran						

  2   4   6   8   10 12

2. How many hats were made altogether?
_____

3. Who made the least number of paper hats?

_____

4. How many more hats did Roxanne make than Edwardo? _____

5. 30 × 7 = 300 – ____

6. Draw a line to divide this shape into two congruent shapes.

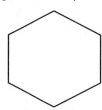

7. My hundred's digit is a 1. My ten's digit is less than 5. My one's digit is zero. What numbers could I be?

____   ____   ____   ____

8. Use mental math to solve these problems.

6 + 2 + 4 + 8 + 9 + 1 = ____

3 + 6 + 4 + 7 + 8 + 2 = ____

9 + 6 + 1 + 4 + 7 + 3 = ____

9.

$$9{,}128 \times 5$$ $$5.89 - 1.95$$ $$7\overline{)420}$$

10. Finish the patterns.

A, C, E, ___, ___, ___

1½, 2½, ____, ____, ____

Exercise 54

1. There are 20 students in the classroom. Ten of the students are girls. Which figure shows how many boys and girls are in the class?

2. Half the girls are in the band. How many girls will leave for band practice?

____

Two-fifths (2/5) of the boys are in band. How many boys will leave for band practice? ____

3. Altogether how many girls and boys will be out of the room for band practice?

_____

What fraction of the total class is this?

$$\overline{20}$$

4. How many hands long is the line?

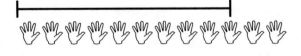

5. What is the area and perimeter of this rectangle?

A = ____

P = ____

10 ft.

5 ft.

6. 240 ÷ ____ = 30

7. Continue the pattern.

53, 51, 49, ____, ____, ____

The rule is _____ .

8. Add two things that could belong in this set.

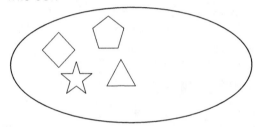

The rule is _____

9.
12.86
+14.29

1,469
– 188

10. Complete this chart.

1/10 of $1.00	10¢
3/10 of $1.00	
5/10 of $1.00	
7/10 of $1.00	
9/10 of $1.00	
1/10 of $2.00	

Exercise 55

1. Monique, David, and Andy each earned 15 stickers for good behavior. How many stickers did they earn all together? _____ stickers

2. They can trade in 20 stickers for $1.00. If they combine their stickers, how much money can they get?

   _____

3. It takes Jamie 20 minutes to get home. If he leaves at 2:05 p.m. what time will he get home? ____:____

   He can run and get home in half the time. What time will he get home if he runs? ____:____

4. Complete the analogy.

   102 : 1020 :: 345 : ____

   a. 3445   **b.** 3450   **c.** 3405

5. Estimate an answer.

   29
   ×6   about 760   200   180

6. Circle $\frac{1}{4}$ of the pigs.

   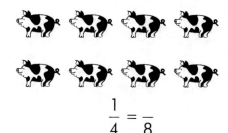

   $\frac{1}{4} = \frac{}{8}$

7. Draw all the lines of symmetry.

8. What is the perimeter of this object?

   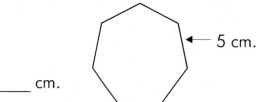

   5 cm.

   ____ cm.

9. The seats in the gym are lettered A through H. Row A has 20 seats. Row B has 22 seats. Row C has 24 seats. How many seats are in row H? _____

10. How many seats does the gym have altogether? _____

1. Tucker blew up 36 balloons. He wanted to share them equally with his sister and brother. How many balloons will they each get?

_____ Tucker _____ brother _____ sister

2. It took Tucker 20 minutes to blow up a dozen balloons. How much time did it take him to blow up all the balloons?

_____ minutes = _____ hours

3. Draw two congruent shapes that each have at least 4 sides.

4. Put these numbers in order of least to greatest.

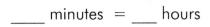
$3\frac{1}{2}$ $3\frac{1}{8}$ $3\frac{1}{4}$ $3\frac{3}{8}$

_____ _____ _____ _____

5.
$$\begin{array}{r} 1{,}628 \\ +423 \\ \hline \end{array}$$
$$\begin{array}{r} 122 \\ \times\ 4 \\ \hline \end{array}$$
$$3\overline{)183}$$

6. You are buying drinks for the school carnival. You need one 2-liter bottle for every 4 people. How many bottles do you need to buy for 500 people?

_____ bottles

7. If only 400 people come, how many bottles will be left over?
_____ bottles

8. Write the geometric names of each figure.

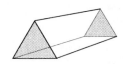

_____ _____

9. Finish the drawing to make a symmetrical shape.

10. Trina is raising insects for her science project. The first day she has 2 insects. The second day she has 4, and the third she has 8. At this rate how many insects will she have on the sixth day?

_____ insects

Exercise 57

Name _____

1. Hui Ling went to the store to buy an ice cream cone. The ice cream cone cost 59¢. How much did she give the clerk if she got 16¢ change?

_____ ¢

....

2. Complete the chart.

hours	minutes
1	
2	
3	
5	

Daily Temperature

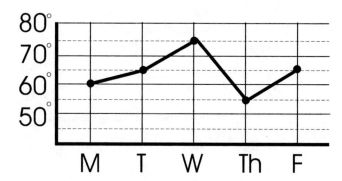

3. What was the temperature on Tuesday?

_____ °

4. How much warmer was it on Wednesday than on Thursday? _____ °

5. If the weather forecast is for the temperature to drop 15° between Friday and Saturday, what temperature will it be on Saturday? _____ °

6. Find the area and perimeter.

6 cm

4 cm

area _____   perimeter _____

....

7. = $5.98   = 1.99

About how much will it cost to buy 2 cans of paint and 1 paint brush?

a. $20.00   b. $14.00   c. $18.00

....

8. Estimate the product.

$$\begin{array}{r} 49 \\ \times 11 \\ \hline \end{array}$$ about   550   250   450

....

9.
$$\begin{array}{r} 1{,}156 \\ +2{,}259 \\ \hline \end{array}$$
$$\begin{array}{r} 429 \\ -237 \\ \hline \end{array}$$
$$\begin{array}{r} 152 \\ \times\ 4 \\ \hline \end{array}$$

....

10. Ray, Bob and Lynn each have a stamp collection. Ray has more than Lynn. Lynn has more than Bob. Put them in order according to the number of stamps they have.

most _____

middle _____

least _____

Exercise 58

1. Nick bought 28 fish. He already had 14 fish. He wanted to divide the fish evenly between two tanks. How many fish will he have in each tank?

_____ fish in each tank

2. Complete the analogy.

150 : 300 :: 1.5 : ____

a. 30.5   b. 3   c. 3.5

3. It is 3:00 p.m. when Jake leaves school. It takes him 10 minutes to get home, 12 minutes to eat a snack, 5 minutes to change his clothes and 13 minutes to walk to the park. Can he make the soccer practice at 4:00 p.m.?

_____

4. Estimate the product.

28
×21   about 500   600   700

5. Draw a picture to show $\frac{5}{9} + \frac{1}{9}$.

6. Complete the pattern.

1, 2, 4, 7, ___, ___, ___, ___

The rule is _____.

7. Round these to the thousands place.

932,681   461,243

_____   _____

8. Complete the chart.

games	played	won	lost
Cubs	100	67	
Tigers	100		15

Using this data, if the Cubs played the Tigers, which team will most likely win? _____

9.
1,850
×   9

5)2135

1,324
−985

10. How many faces and vertices does this prism have?

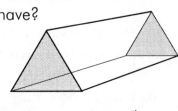

_____ faces   _____ vertices

Exercise 59

Name _____

1. Catalina has 55¢. She finds 2 quarters. She spends 10¢. How much money does Catalina have now?

____¢

·······································

2. Write multiplication problems for these arrays.

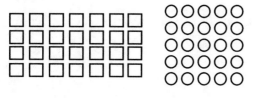

_____ _____

·······································

3. 1 minute = ____ seconds

3 minutes = ____ seconds

·······································

4. Jude and his friends ate 6 pieces of the pizza. What fraction of the pizza was left?

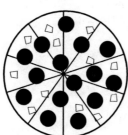

_____ left

·······································

5. Write the names of the objects below.

_____ _____

6. Complete this drawing to make a symmetrical figure.

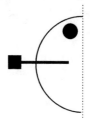

·······································

7. Insert <, =, or > to make this a true number sentence.

4 × 160 ◯ 600 + 50 + 4

·······································

8. Match these fractions with equal decimals.

___ 3 5/10   a. 3.555

___ 3 55/100   b. 3.5

___ 3 555/1000   c. 3.55

·······································

9. 475   6662   4)‾2005‾
      −386   +3504

·······································

10. Draw a parallelogram.

If two of the sides are 4 cm. and two of the sides are 2 cm., what is the perimeter? _____

Exercise 60

1. Adriana needs to be home by 6:00 p.m. It takes her 15 minutes to walk home. What time should she leave her friend's house?

_____:_____

2. Write these fractions from smallest to largest.

$$\frac{1}{5} \qquad \frac{1}{2} \qquad \frac{1}{3}$$

_____ _____ _____

3. Write the set of even numbers that are greater than 7 but less than 19.

{ ___, ___, ___, ___, ___, ___ }

4. Draw an scalene triangle and a right triangle.

5. Are these letters symmetrical?

T   **F**   **O**

_____ _____ _____

6. Circle the odd numbers. Then write the odd numbers in order from least to greatest.

3,689   3,688   3,685
3,638   3,692   3,691

_____ _____ _____

7. Show how you would divide $1.46 into two equal amounts.

8. $9\overline{)4563}$ $5\overline{)4890}$

9.
8,282	$3.75	415
−4,224	+1.63	× 5

10. Todd's pack weighs more than Jaime's but less than Killeen's. Draw a line to match each person with his or her backpack.

Todd	11 pounds
Jaime	10 pounds
Killeen	8 pounds

© 2005 Prufrock Press Inc   Math Warm-Ups Grade 3

Exercise 61

Name _____

1. Rachel has 3 fish. Two of the fish each had 2 babies. How many fish does she have now? Draw a picture and write a number sentence.

....

2. Complete the analogy.

89 : 890 :: 34 : ____

a. 340   **b.** 430   **c.** 440

....

3. Cara had $1.60. She worked for her mother for 3 hours and got 50¢ per hour. How much does she have now?

_____

....

4. Finish the pattern.

4:05, 4:15, 4:25, _____, _____

The rule is _____.

....

5. Round to the nearest hundred.

4,067 _____   1,406 _____

1,167 _____   519 _____

6. Put in order from least to greatest.

14.66   13.33   14.23   13.65

_____ _____ _____ _____

....

7. Find the area and the perimeter of the object shown.

4 in.

perimeter_____   area_____

....

8. 3 × 14 = ___ + ___ + ___

4 × 33 = ___ + ___ + ___ + ___

....

9. Fill in the missing points on the number line.

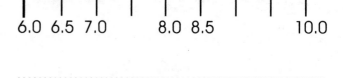

6.0 6.5 7.0   8.0 8.5   10.0

....

10. Draw and label an obtuse angle and an acute angle.

Exercise 62

Bicycle Ride

Rafael	🚲 🚲
Antonio	🚲 🚲 🚲 🚲 🚲
Luke	🚲

🚲 = 3 miles

1. Each person needs to ride 15 miles to complete the course. How many more miles does Rafael need to ride?

_____ miles

2. How many more miles does Antonio need to ride to reach 15 miles?

_____ miles

3. How many more miles did Antonio ride than Luke?

_____ more miles

....

4. Complete the analogy.

$1.45 : $2.55 :: $6.30 : _____

a. $7.60   **b.** $7.40   **c.** $6.35

....

5. 3×7 = ___ + ___ + ___ = ___

3×70 = ___ + ___ + ___ = ___

3×77 = ___ + ___ + ___ = ___

6. The circus starts at 3:00 p.m. It takes Chris 20 minutes to get to the circus. When does Chris have to leave?

_____:_____ p.m.

....

7. Write the value of each coin if the total value of all the coins is $1.46

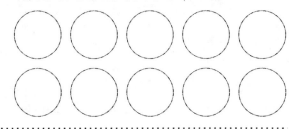

8. Finish the fact family.

30×4 = _____

___ × ___ = _____

$120 \div$ ___ = ___

___ ÷ ___ = ___

....

9.
$$1,638 \qquad 5,764 \qquad 4\overline{)280}$$
$$-1,244 \qquad +\ 936$$

....

10. If you continue this pattern, what would be the twelfth letter be _____?

A, B, B, C, C, C, _____

Exercise 63

1. Francisco has 3 different colored socks (1 blue, 1 red, and 1 white). He has two pairs of shoes (1 black and 1 brown). Show all the different combinations he can make.

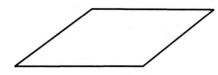

....

2. Complete the analogy.

22 : 44 :: 55 : ___

a. 99   b. 110   c. 66

....

3. Name this figure and write two facts about it.

_____

_____

....

4. Circle the odd numbers that are divisible by 5.

105   124   125   120   136

Write three more odd numbers greater than 100 that are divisible by 5.

____   ____   ____

5. Finish the pattern.

200, 175, 150, _____, _____

....

6. If this is 1/3 of the total number of bones in the box, how many bones are in the box? _____ bones

....

7. If you divided 180 paperclips into 6 equal piles, how many would be in each pile?

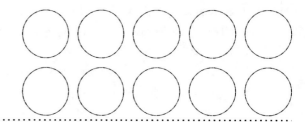

____ paperclips

....

8. The value of all the coins equals 83¢. Write the value of each coin.

○ ○ ○ ○ ○

○ ○ ○ ○ ○

....

9. (70 − 25) + 9 = ___

(4 + 5) × 30 = ___

....

10. List all the numbers between 80 and 100 that are divisible by 3.

____   ____   ____

____   ____   ____

Exercise 64

Name _____

1. Verlene shot 10 baskets that counted for 2 points each and 6 baskets that counted for 3 points each. How many points did she score in the basketball game?

_____ points

2. Complete the analogy.

triangle : 3 :: hexagon : _____

3. What would you use to measure the weight of a puppy?

gallons   inches   pounds

4. What would you use to measure the length of the hallway in your school?

inches   feet   miles

5. Write these decimals as fractions.

example $.2 = \dfrac{2}{10}$ $.22 = \dfrac{22}{100}$

$.5 =$

$.75 =$

$.575 =$

6. If $A = 15$

$A + A + A + A = $ _____

7. Draw a picture and shade 3/4. Finish the number sentence.

$$\frac{4}{4} - \frac{3}{4} =$$

8.  = $4.95   = $24.95

About how much would it cost to buy a pair of sunglasses and a watch?

a. $30.00   b. $35.00 $40.00

9.
$$\begin{array}{ccc} 300 & 15 & 315 \\ \times\ 3 & \times 3 & \times\ 3 \end{array}$$

10. What is the volume of this figure if each side is equal to 3 centimeters?

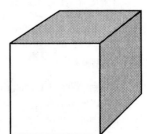

_____ cubic cm.

Exercise 65

1. Shawn and his two friends want to have some soup. One can makes 2 bowls. How many cans of soup will Shawn need to make so that they each get one bowl?

_____ cans

2. Write a mixed number for the shaded part.

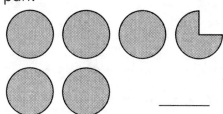

_____

3. A recipe for punch calls for 2 quarts of lemonade. Wade only has a cup measure. How many cups of lemonade should he use?

_____ cups

4. If you repeat this pattern, what will the tenth figure be?

★ ☆ ☆ ✪

5. Circle the numbers that are divisible by both 2 and 5.

200   **205**   **2,215**

6. Round these numbers to the nearest thousand.

991 _____   2,634 _____

1,091 _____   1,444 _____

7. Continue the pattern.

.1, .3, .5, ____, ____, ____

8. 3 × 16 = ____ = 4 × ____

9.

```
  41          1.48        1,691
  42         -.39        ×    5
 +18
```

10. How many grams would you add to the right side to balance the scale?

Exercise 66

1. Brad wants to buy two balls that are $5.95 each. He gives the clerk $20.00. How much money should he get back?

$_____

....

2. Complete the analogy.

thousand : hundred :: 1,000 : _____

....

3. Complete this figure so it is symmetric.

....

4. Write the numeral for **one hundred twenty thousand two hundred eighty-eight**.

_____

....

5. Olivia baked 55 cookies for the bake sale. Nora baked twice as many cookies. How many cookies were baked in all?

_____ cookies

6. This is 2/6 of the flies.

How many flies are there altogether?

....

7. If ● = 9, what is 13 × ● ?

....

8. These are the toys in Justin's toy box.

If he chooses without looking will he be more likely to get a truck, motorcycle, plane or boat?

_____

....

9.

$$\begin{array}{r} 49 \\ + \\ \hline 53 \end{array} \qquad \begin{array}{r} 1158 \\ -375 \\ \hline \end{array} \qquad 7\overline{)147}$$

....

10. Hector is 4 years younger than Jill. Jill is 18 years old. Chang is older than Hector but younger than Jill. What ages could Chang be?

_____   _____   _____

Exercise 67

1. It takes Yoshi 20 minutes to walk to school. She needs to be at school by 8:00 a.m. What time should she leave home?

____:____ a.m.

2. Write an ordered pair to describe the location of points A and B.

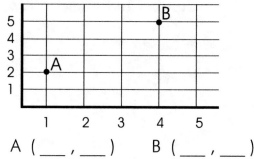

A (___ , ___)   B (___ , ___)

3. Estimate the product.

$\begin{array}{r} 67 \\ \times 9 \\ \hline \end{array}$ about   500   600   800

4. Write the names of these figures.

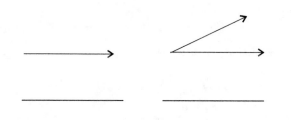

_____   _____

5. Insert <, =, or > to make this a true number sentence.

3.5 ⬭ 3.53

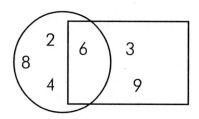

6. The numbers in the circle are multiples of ___.

7. The numbers in the rectangle are multiples of ___.

8. The number in the circle and the rectangle is a multiple of ____.

9.
$\begin{array}{r} 126 \\ +74 \\ \hline \end{array}$ $\begin{array}{r} 6{,}923 \\ -2{,}744 \\ \hline \end{array}$ $\begin{array}{r} 842 \\ \times 7 \\ \hline \end{array}$

10. All of these figures have perimeters of 36 cm. What are the measures of one of their sides?

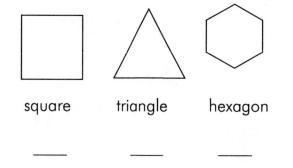

square   triangle   hexagon

_____   _____   _____

Exercise 68

Name _____

1. Liam bought a DVD for $15.96. How much change should he get back from $20.00? _____

How much more money does he need to purchase another DVD for $15.96?

_____

2. If the radius of this circle is 4 centimeters, the diameter is _____ cm.

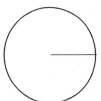

3. Divide this figure into equal parts and shade it to show 3/5.

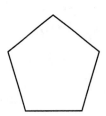

4. If school gets out at 2:30 and baseball practice starts at 5:15, how much time is there between school and practice?

_____ hour _____ minutes

5.
```
  8,961
×     4
```
8)488

6.
```
  2,345          7,897
+1,567         −5,988
```

7. Make a graph that shows the number of people present in your room each day during the last week.

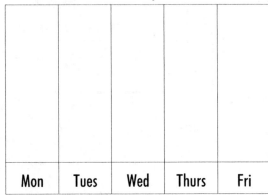

Number of People in Class

Mon	Tues	Wed	Thurs	Fri

8. How many people were absent on each day?

___ ___ ___ ___ ___
M   T   W   Th   F

9. Insert <, =, or > to make this a true number sentence.

8,372 ◯ 8,000 + 399

10. Room 4 has 25 students. Room 5 has 27 students. What is the average number of students in both classes?

_____ students

Name _____

1. Luke has ten bills in his drawer. He has two $5 bills, three $10 bills and the rest are $20 bills. Which one is he most likely to pull out if he reaches in without looking?

_____

2. Write two true number sentences using the numbers 5, 15, and 75.

_____

_____

3. Identify the angles below as acute, obtuse and right.

_____

_____

_____

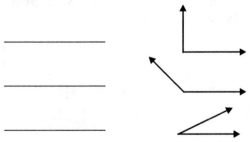

4. Stephen has $5.00. Hot dogs are 49¢ each. How many hot dogs can he buy if he uses all his money?

_____ hot dogs

5. 7,863
       ×   4

    12)372

6. quadrilateral : perimeter :: circle : __

a. circumference   b. area   c. oval

7.

    18,754   18,754
    + 189   − 189

8. Write a decimal and a fraction for **four wholes and six hundredths.**

_____   _____

9. These are Michael's grades in history: 99, 96, 76, 89 and 90. Find his average for the semester.

_____

10.   **Math Test Scores**

	4th grade	5th grade	6th grade
this year	487	499	461
last year	423	470	489

Which class had the greatest increase in math scores from last year to this year?

_____ grade

Exercise 70

Sun	Mon	Tues	Wed	Thur	Fri	Sat
		1	2	3	4	5
6	7	8	9	10	11	12
13	14	15	16	17	18	19
20	21	22	23	24	25	26
27	28	29	30			

1. Mr. Chu only wears his Hawaiian tie on Wednesdays that are multiples of 3. What dates this month will he wear his Hawaiian tie?

_____

2. It takes 3 weeks for Brad to finish his book. If he started reading on the third day of the month, on what date will he finish? _____

3. Mrs. Olivera starts reading a story on the second day of the month and reads a chapter every other day (Monday through Friday). If the book has 12 chapters will she finish before the end of the month?

_____

4.
$$4{,}688 + 1{,}501 \qquad 4{,}688 - 1{,}501$$

5. Correct the mistake in the pattern.

450, 439, 429, 417, 406

The rule is _____

6.
$$\begin{array}{r} 146 \\ \times\ 9 \\ \hline \end{array} \qquad 9\overline{)135} \qquad \begin{array}{r} 3.75 \\ +4.57 \\ \hline \end{array}$$

7. 1 hour = ____ minutes

1/2 hours = ____ minutes

1/3 hour = ____ minutes

8. Write the numeral for **six hundred eighteen thousand, two hundred thirty-six**

_____

9. Put these fractions in order from smallest to largest.

$$\frac{7}{10} \qquad \frac{4}{10} \qquad \frac{6}{10} \qquad \frac{12}{10}$$

____ ____ ____ ____

10. Write a decimal for the shaded part.

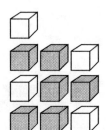

____

Answers

Exercise 1, pg. 5
1. Sunday, October 26th
2. yes
3. $15.00
4. b. 60 ~~or 50~~
5. <
6. 8
7. 73, 75, 77
8. 8:25
9. 50 49 60 59
10. circle, triangle

Exercise 2, pg 6
1. 13¢, 20¢
2. 7¢
3. 1:30
4. a. 65
5. 1 dime = 10¢
   2 dimes = 20¢
   6 dimes = 60¢
6. 4   4   0
7. shade 4 doughnuts
   >
8. 23 25 99 97
9. 64   19   50
10. 44

Exercise 3
1. bar graph showing the same information as the tally.
2. Chase
3. 1
4. 6/10
5. 1:00
6. larger black circle
7. 142 234 369 432
8. square   rectangle
9. 343   84   24
10. 7 + 7 + 7 + 7

Exercise 4, pg. 8
1. 5, 2
2. 6
3. 4
4. no, You will be late by 5 minutes.
5. 10,922
6. 1 quarter + 5 dimes
7. b. Sunday
8. 265   124   40
9. 6 + 6 = 12
10. yellow
    There is a larger portion of yellow than blue.

Exercise 5, pg. 9
1. b. 10 minutes
2. 11:35
3. 200
   300
4. 2 x 6   4 x 3
5. 6 sides   6 vertices
6. yes
7. 12, 10, 8
   rule - subtract 2
8. 2   0   4
   420   910   150
9. 100   125   150
10. 7

Exercise 6, pg. 10
1. drawing showing 4 apples per person
2. 32 ounces or 2 pounds
   96 ounces or 6 pounds
3. 2 and 5
4. upside down unshaded star
5. 5 lines of symmetry
6. 63¢
7. 65, 70, 75, 80, 85, 90
   rule - add 5
8. 75   90   30
9. 4 + 4 + 4 = 12
   3 + 3 + 3 + 3
10. 675   533

Exercise 7, pg. 11
1. 88
2. Students should correctly draw a radius.
3. 3 × 9 = 27
4. 1057, 1056
5. 8   80   70
   700
6. 40   60   120
7. pentagon 5   oval 0
8. circle the circle
9.
10. >

Exercise 8, pg. 12
1. 30 minutes
2. 12 days
3. 3:50 p.m.
4. 8
5. 6 squares, 2 rows , 3 in each row pattern - add one square
6. 18, 20, 22
7. 50 + 30
8. =
9. 360   180   100
10. Circle should be divided into thirds and one sections shaded.

Exercise 9, pg. 13
1. $.25
2. 60 minutes or 1 hour
   Jake
3. 300 + 40 + 5
4. circle on left shows 5/6
5. There are 2 lines of symmetry, one horizontal and one vertical.
6. 4   2
7. line should be horizontal and parallel to Main St.
8. 40 37 24 240
9. a
10. 2x8 - most fence (a)
    3x6 - largest inside (b)

Exercise 10, pg. 14
1. $3.00 $15.00
2. fill in the numbers 1.5 and 2.5
3. 9 10 11 12 13
4. $1.00 $2.00
5. 6 ½ units
6. The cone should be circled.
7. 6,963
8. 100   90
   80   90
9. 5   40   39
10. The square should be divided into 4 parts and 2 parts should be shaded.
    2/4 or 1/2

Exercise 11, pg. 15
1. 27   5
2. won 7/12 lost 5/12
3. won 12/15 3/15
4. 6/10
5. 1364   1396   1989
6. 24 - 18 = 6 or 24 - 18 = 6
   6 + 18 = 24 or 18 + 6 = 24
7. 9   1   4
   3400   800   900
8. 52   48   38
9. $3\frac{1}{2}$
10. 6 × 1

Exercise 12, pg. 16
1. 8
2. 6
3. 26
4. 6 faces   8 vertices
5. clock showing 3:55
6. 5
7. 47, 49, 51
   rule - add 2
8. =
9. 82   12   26
10. 1 vertical line of symmetry

Exercise 13, pg. 17
1. $1.08
2. 2
3. 66   82   24
4. The right side of the drawing should be a mirror image of the drawing that is supplied in the problem.
5. a. bcd
6. sphere
7. answers will vary
8. >
9. 199, 200, 201
   rule - add 1
10. $7.00

Exercise 14, pg. 18
1. Steven   3¢
2. 2 × 4
3. .3   7/10   .9
4. 45 minutes
5. a. 12 × 2 d. 10 + 10 + 4
6. Students should draw two congruent right triangles.
7. line of symmetry for each polygon
8. 18   510   32
9. 122, 112, 102
10. yes

Exercise 15, pg. 19
1. 14
2. 6
3. 1
4. c. 10 + 5
5. 1,687
6. 1501   619   48
7. No, they are different sizes.
8. 3,000   8,000   5,000
9. >
10. line segment

Exercise 16, pg. 16
1. 18
2. shortest distance, 4 blocks
3. 6 routes
4. $1\frac{1}{2}$ inches
5. about $1.60
6. cylinder
7. drawing of a right triangle
8. 75   390   400
9. 6,803
10. Shannon (oldest)
    Connor
    Allison (youngest)

Exercise 17, pg. 21
1. Jill - 45¢ Sarah - 55¢
2. Sarah 10¢
3. a and b
   b. pentagon
4. 20, 24, 28, 32
   rule - add 4
5. 4 + 4
6. 600   602   604
7. 2/4 or 1/2   1/6
8. 72   73   74
9. blue
10. blue - 12/75 yellow - 15/75
    red - 20/75 brown - 28/75

Exercise 18, pg. 22
1. 15
   picture of 3 groups of 5
2. 1/6
3. 3 × 4
4. about 1.50
5. 144,093
6. 84   8   140
7. $1\frac{2}{3}$ $2\frac{1}{3}$
8. 4 cubic units
9. 4 sets with 4 in each set
   16 ÷ 4 = 4
10. $200

Exercise 19, pg. 22
1. taco
2. 10
3. 10
4. 3 quarters, 1 dime, 2 nickels, 1 penny
5. 20 ÷ 2
6. 3   28   160
7. 180, 200
8. 40 cubic in.
9. >
10.

Exercise 20, pg. 24
1. 100
2. 30 out of 100
3. a. 112
4. $2\frac{1}{4}$
5. 7 13 17
6. 250,651
7. 200, 230
8. 70   70
   170   1,170
9. 7:25
10. 70°

Exercise 21, pg. 25
1. 14
2. 4
3. 4:50
4. 2/6 or 1/3 6/10 or 3/5
5. 8 ÷ 2
   answers will vary (sum = 15)
6. 3 × 2 = 6   6 ÷ 2 = 3
   2 × 3 = 6   6 ÷ 3 = 2
7. 5   11   25
8. 102 110 122 150
9. 69   1,018   88
10. 4/10   8/10
    34/100 25/100

Exercise 22, pg. 26
1. meter
2. Tracy - 99 lbs   Marcus - 98 lbs
3. b. 6
4. answers will vary
5. 5 × 9 = 45   45 ÷ 5 = 9
   9 × 5 = 45   45 ÷ 9 = 5
6. 400
7. 24   7   10
8. 12 cups 2 cups
9. 1000   8800   1600
10. 2/10 shaded   8/10 unshaded

Exercise 23, pg. 27
1. 4 boxes (3 full boxes and 1 box with 9 dolls)
2. 1:10
3. a. 930
4. a. 35 - 3
5. 317, 324, 332
6. 7 × 8 = 56   56 ÷ 7 = 8
   8 × 7 = 56   56 ÷ 8 = 7
7. 100   73   200
8. 180
9. 2 5 0 2
10. Need to know how much money Megan has.

Exercise 24, pg. 28
1. 1:35 p.m.
2. 12 ÷ 4 = 3
3. any expression equal to 13; answers will vary
4. answers will vary; some possibilities are:
   3 - 25¢ = 75¢
   2 - 25¢ + 1 - 10¢ = 60¢
   2 - 25¢ + 1 - 5¢ = 80¢
5. 12 × 4
6. 721   h = 7, t = 2
  684   h = 6, t = 8
 6884   h = 8, t = 8
7. 700   700   6,900
8. 4/6 3/6 circle 4/6
9. 98   72   108
10. 40 miles

Exercise 25, pg. 29
1. 38
2. clock showing 5:10
3. 20 × 1
4. vertical symmetry - A H M O T U V W X
  horizontal symmetry - D E H I O X
5. two parallelograms with different angles or side lengths
6. 2,000   1,000
  2,000   2,000
7. insert the fractions 2/5 3/5
8. shade 1/8 unshaded 7/8
9. 1501   4   120
10. 188, 208, 228
  rule - add 20

Exercise 26, pg. 30
1. 19 seconds
2. 5 feet 4 inches
3. Lily
  Matt
  Dora
  Joey
4. circle divided into 4 parts with 3/4 shaded
5. 2.90, 3.20
  rule - add .30
6. 3 × 4
7. 9,000   3,000   2,000
8. 298   299   301
  302
9. 33   91   21
10. 1 - 50¢ and 2 - 1¢

Exercise 27, pg. 31
1. 100
2. 20
3. answers will vary
4. G7
5. 8:15
6. graph correctly labeled with points (2,3) and (4,3)
7. 145   11
8. 8 units
9. 7/10, 9/10, 11,10
10. 18   45
   27   54
   36   63

Exercise 28, pg. 32
1. b. 300
2. Thursday
3. a. 150
4. 6:30
5. pyramid
6. 81 - 10 + 6 = 77
7. 20 - 5
8. thermometer shaded to show 76°
9. 109   121   203
10. DDD   DDN   DDP
   DPP   DNN   DNP
   NNN   NNP
   PPP   PPN

Exercise 29, pg 33
1. 11:34 a.m.
2. four sides; two of the sides are parallel
3. 1 - 25¢, 5 - 10¢, 2 - 5¢, 2 - 1¢
4. $6.55
5. drawing should show 2 parallel lines with a diagonal line that intersects each line.
6. 5,000   7,000
  2,000   10,000
7. 5, 5½, 6
  rue - add 1/2
8. 25
9. 447   105   6
10. drawing should show shaded = 5/12 unshaded = 7/12

Exercise 30, pg. 34
1. 9; 3
2. 1 hour 15 minutes
3. 1.00, 1.25, 1.50
4. 1 - 50¢   2 - 25¢
  4 - 10¢   2 - 5¢   1 - 1¢
5. P = 16   P = 12
  A = 15   A = 8
6. >
7. 24 things divided into 3 groups with 8 in each group
8. A →
9. 519   469   14 r 4
10. 1.0   2.00   3.00

Exercise 31, pg. 35
1. 2 cupcakes
2. 2.1 2.2 2.3 2.4
3. $36.25
4. 1,523 1,686 1,846 1,943
5. >
6. vertical line perpendicular to the horizontal line
7. a. ray
  b. line segment
  c. line
8. 3 × 3
9. 256   6   23
10. 21

Exercise 32, pg. 36
1. 70 pounds
2. 60 pounds
3. 50 pounds
4. b
5. b. quart
6. 5/7   3/7   circle 5/7
7. 10¢
8. 30 ÷ 2
9. 116   306   8
10. 10 miles

Exercise 33, pg. 37
1. 75   15
2. yes
3. 7
4. $3 \times 7 = 21$ $21 \div 3 = 7$
   $7 \times 3 = 21$ $21 \div 7 = 3$
5. 5½
6. 10 × 14
7. 2000   2500   3000
8. <
9. 320   320   16
10. 20 miles

Exercise 34, pg. 38
1. 8
2. $4.80
3. a. 18
4. drawing of a radius and diameter
5. 1800
6. circle 12 cupcakes
7. yes; 6 left over
8. 10 + 10
9. $5.44 $3.02 $7.05
10. Ellie

Exercise 35, pg. 38
1. Bar graph with the following squares labeled and shaded:
   Juan - shade 4
   Travis - shade 6
   Miguel - shade 4
   Brent - shade 3
2. 2
3. no; Juan + Miguel = 8
   Travis + Brent = 9
4. 40 points
5. $45 \div 5 = 9$ or $45 \div 9 = 5$
   $72 \div 6 = 12$ or $72 \div 12 = 6$
   $105 \div 7 = 15$ or
   $105 \div 15 = 7$
6. shade 6 blimps
7. 3/4   1/4
   6/8   2/8
8. 144 ÷ 12
9. 1,259   18r1   3,354
10. 8   8   1

Exercise 36, pg. 40
1. 5
2. 2 thousands 3 hundreds 7 tens 6 ones
3. pentagon   octagon
4. $175.00
5. $75.00
6. .75 1.25 1.5 1.75
7. $70 $105 $175
8. $3 \times 2 \times 7$
9. $.99 $2.22 $1.32
10. circle 4   circle 5
   2,000   3,000

Exercise 37, pg. 41
1. Tom - 16
   Mary - 12
   Chad - 17
   total - 45
2. 15
3. 3:25 p.m.
4. 56, 60, 64
5. 33 36 39 42
   44 48 52 56
   55 60 65 70
6. first square - shade 2 sections
   second square - shade 2 sections
   third square - shade 4 sections
7. $1.50 $8.20
   $1.10 $1.30
8. 2 - 50¢ 1 - 10¢ 1 - 1¢
9. 127   60   42
10. NNN   NNP   NND
   NPP   NDD

Exercise 38, pg. 42
1. 4
2. 20th
3. Thursday, February 8
4. three
5. 7 - 25¢ 2 - 10¢ 1 - 5¢
6. >
7. hexagon   parallelogram
8. $2 \times (3 \times 4) = 24$
9. 212   242   33
10. 6,000   2,000
   7,000   2,000

Exercise 39, pg. 43
1. tally should show girls canvas = 6
   leather = 14
   boys canvas = 8 leather = 12
2. bar graph should have four bars (2 for girls and 2 for boys) that show:
   girls canvas = 6 leather = 14
   boys canvas = 8 leather = 12
3. 26/40
4. 2
5. circle 2 cars   8/10
6. 54 cm.
7. 800 + 40 + 5
8. 32 × 3
9. 2410 $1.59   70
10. 45

Exercise 40, pg. 44
1. 2 hamburgers and 1 ice cream or 1 hamburger and 4 ice creams or 7 ice creams
2. 11:00 a.m. 3:00 p.m. 7:00 p.m.
3. 3/4
4. drawing should show two figures that are the same shape and size.
   examples - right triangle, square, rectangle
5. 3 ounces
6. answers will vary
7. 3 units
8. 95
9. 16   240   256
10. 280 + 960 = 1240
   130 + 810 = 940
   300 + 190 = 490

Exercise 41, pg. 45
1. 20 people
2. 4 more people
3. 2 pizzas
4. shade 10 cats
5. 5/9
6. 8/10, 10/10, 12/10
   rule - add 2/10
7. oval is not a polygon
8. 6/10   8/100
9. 20¢   70¢
10. Danielle
   Amy
   Tasha
   Jill

Exercise 42, pg. 46
1. 18 fish; 6 fish each
2. 9 11 13 15; 15 fish
3. 4 8 16 32; 32 hours
4. 203
5. 1,200,040
6. 100   2,300
   1,200   400
7. $4.35
8. 3 + 57
9. 16   160   3/10
10. drawings should show the fractions 1/4 and 1/6

Exercise 43, pg. 47
1. $38.37
2. 90
3. b. 48
4. 3 ½ units
5. 4¾
6. shade 3 faces
   3/8 + 5/8 = 8/8
7. =
8. 40   200   240
9. 5 cups = 2 pints + 1 cup
10. JTH   JHT   TJH
    THJ   HTJ   HJT

Exercise 44, pg. 48
1. 16 20 24   24 minutes
2. 6 feet 4 inches
3. 7 hours
4. answers will vary
5. 35, 45, 55
6. $2.04 $2.40 $2.50 $2.55
7. 18 pieces
8. 15   150   165
9. 50   49   48
10. February, March

Exercise 45, pg. 49
1. 67
2. 7 squares 9 squares
3. 3:10 p.m.
4. 1,000
5. cylinder, prism
6. shade 2 sections 2/8 + 6/8
   = 8/8
7. answers will vary
8. 22   19,036   95
9. 2 × 9
10. no   yes   yes

Exercise 46, pg. 50
1. 18
2. $180.00 $170.00
3. 10   20
   12   24
   20   40
4. 14
5. 4
6. 8 × 4 = 32   32 ÷ 4 = 8
   4 × 8 = 32   32 ÷ 8 = 4
7. 10,000
8. 10 minutes
   6 reports
9. 81   100   20 R 3
10. QPQ   QPP
    QPN   QPD
    More combinations are possible if one uses a half dollar coin or a dollar coin.

Exercise 47, pg. 51
1. graph should be shaded the following way:
   coconut - 2 ½ squares
   sugar - 1 square
   chocolate - 3 squares
   peanut butter - 1½ squares
   vanilla - 1 square
2. 18 votes
3. 3
4. yes;   answers will vary
5. 48 legs
6. 633, 643, 653
7. Shape should match the one that is provided.
8. 2 × 2 × 2 × 2 × 2 × 2
9. 109   728   9014
10. 6 to the left side

Exercise 48, pg. 52
1. Sept. 25th
2. 18 days
3. Assuming that school starts on the week of the 7th, there are 4 days; September 8th, 10th, 22nd, and 24th
4. 3 5 7
5. 90
6. 43 21
7. 15 cm.
8. 15 bananas
9. 1 out of 5 or 1/5 or 2/10
10. .50 .75 1.00 2.00

Exercise 49, pg. 53
1. 2 seconds
2. at least 40 seconds
3. points should be labeled correctly on the grid
4. answers will vary
5. 5000 + 300 + 40 + 6
6. 27 36 45 54 63 72 81
   24 32 40 48 56 64 72
7. right triangle, equilateral triangle
8. 80   1200   1600
9. 3.1 3.2 3.3 3.4
10. $14.50 $68.05

Exercise 50, pg. 54
1. 10 chopsticks
2. b. 84
3. 5:50
4. each person gets $10.25
5. 10.05 10.09 10.50 10.90
6. circles should show 3/6 shaded and 4/8 shaded
   3/6 = 4/8
7. 45.5, 50.5, 55.5
8. 36 ÷ 2
9. 10,147   6   169
10. turtle snake sheep mouse

Exercise 51, pg. 55
1. 62   124
2. 7:30
3. shade to show 55 degrees
4. circle 4 snowflakes
5. circle the six-sided figure
6. drawing should be a mirror image of what has been provided
7. A = 32 sq. cm.   P = 24 cm.
8. c. liter
9. faces = 5
   edges = 8
   vertices = 5
10. 300   1000   1300

Exercise 52, pg. 56
1. graph should be shaded as follows:
   lemon - 1½ squares shaded
   strawberry - 3 squares shaded
   chocolate - 4 squares shaded
   vanilla - 2 squares shaded
2. 6 pints
3. 8 pints = 4 quarts
4. quarts
5. 41 $1.05
6. shade 2 rectangles 5/5 - 2/5 = 3/5
7. 4 equal sides, 4 right angles, closed figure
8. 22, 24, 26, 28, 40, 42, 44, 46, 48
9. 84   100   416
10. 38   57   76
    40   60   80

Exercise 53, pg. 55
1. shade graph as follows:
   Jose - 12   Roxanne - 11
   Edwardo - 8   Shiran - 10
2. 41
3. Edwardo
4. 3
5. 300 - 90
6. can be divided horizontally or vertically
7. 110 120 130 140
8. 30   30   30
9. 45,640   3.94   60
10. G, I, K
    3½, 4½, 5½

Exercise 54, pg. 58
1. the middle figure
2. 5 girls   4 boys
3. 9   9/20
4. 9 ½ hands
5. A= 50 sq. ft.
   P = 30 ft.
6. 8
7. 47, 45, 43
   rule - subtract 2
8. answers will vary
   closed figures with straight lines; polygons
9. 27.15   1281
10. 30¢
    50¢
    70¢
    90¢
    20¢

Exercise 55, pg. 59
1. 45 stickers
2. $2.00 with 5 stickers left over
3. 2:25 p.m.   2:15 p.m.
4. b. 3450
5. 180
6. circle 2 pigs   1/4 = 2/8
7. The line can be drawn vertically or horizontally through the center of the figure.
8. 35 cm.
9. 34 seats
10. 216 seats

Exercise 56, pg. 60
1. 12   12   12
2. 60 minutes = 1 hour
3. answers will vary
4. 3 ⅛ 3 ¼ 3 ⅜ 3 ½
5. 2,051   488   61
6. 125 bottles
7. 25 bottles left over
8. triangular prism   cone
9. Drawing should be a mirror image of what is provided.
10. 64 insects

Exercise 57, pg. 61
1. 75¢
2. 1   60
   2   120
   3   180
   5   300
3. 65°
4. 20°
5. 50°
6. A = 24 sq. cm.
   P = 20 cm.
7. b. $14.00
8. 550
9. 3415   192   608
10. Ray
    Lynn
    Bob

Exercise 58, pg. 62
1. 21 fish in each tank
2. b. 3
3. yes, he will get there by 3:40 p.m.
4. 600
5. drawing will vary but show 5/9 + 1/9 for a total of 6/9
6. 11, 16, 22, 29
   rule - add 1, add 2, add 3, add 4, add 5, add 6, add 7...
7. 933,000   461,000
8. Cubs   100   67   33
   Tigers   100   85   15
   Tigers
9. 16,650   427   339
10. 5 faces   6 vertices

Exercise 59, pg. 63
1. 95¢
2. 4 x 7   5 x 5
3. 60   180
4. 4/10 left
5. sphere   pyramid
6. drawing should be the mirror image of what is already drawn
7. <
8. b. 3.5
   c. 3.55
   a. 3.555
9. 89   10,166   501 r1
10. perimeter = 12 cm.

Exercise 60, pg. 64
1. 5:45 p.m.
2. 1/5   1/3   1/2
3. 8, 10, 12, 14, 16, 18
4. drawing of a scalene and a right triangle
5. T - yes F - no O - yes
6. 3,685   3,689   3,691
7. $.73 each
8. 507   978
9. 4058   5.38   2075
10. Todd - 10
    Jaime - 8
    Killeen - 11

Exercise 61, pg. 65
1. 7 fish $3 + 2 + 2 = 7$
2. a. 340
3. $3.10
4. 4:35, 4:45
   rule - add 10 minutes
5. 4,100   1,400
   1,200   500
6. 13.33   13.65   14.23   14.66
7. P = 16 sq. in.
   A = 16 in.
8. 14 + 14 + 14
   33 + 33 + 33 + 33
9. 7.5   9.0   9.5
10. picture of an obtuse (greater than 90°) and acute (less that 90°) angle

Exercise 62, pg. 66
1. 9 miles
2. 0 miles
3. 12 miles
4. b. $7.40
5. $7 + 7 + 7 = 21$
   $70 + 70 + 70 = 210$
   $77 + 77 + 77 = 231$
6. 2:40 p.m.
7. 4 - 25¢   4 - 10¢
   1 - 5¢   1- 1¢
8. $30 \times 4 = 120$
   $4 \times 30 = 120$
   $120 \div 4 = 30$
   $120 \div 30 = 4$
9. 394   6700   70
10. E

Exercise 63, pg. 67
1. b-bl   b-br
   r-bl   r-br
   w-bl   w-br
2. b. 110
3. parallelogram
   4 side; opposite sides are equal and parallel; closed figure; opposite angles are equal; a polygon
4. 105   125
   answers will vary
5. 125, 100
6. 24 bones
7. 30 paperclips
8. 1-25¢   5-10¢
   1-5¢   3-1¢
9. 54   270
10. 81   84   87   90   93   96

Exercise 64. pg. 68
1. 38 points
2. 6
3. pounds
4. feet
5. .5 = 5/10   .75 = 75/100
   .575 = 575/1000
6. 60
7. picture showing 3/4   4/4 - 3/4
   = 1/4
8. a. $30.00
9. 900   45   945
10. 27 cu. cm.

Exercise 65 , pg. 69
1. 2 cans
2. 5¾
3. 8 cups
4. ☆
5. 200
6. 1,000   3,000
   1,000   1,000
7. .7   .9   1.1
8. $48 = 4 \times 12$
9. 101   1.09   8,455
10. 1.5 grams

Exercise 66, pg. 70
1. $8.10
2. 100
3. Figure should horizontally reflect what has been drawn.
4. 120,288
5. 165 cookies
6. 18 flies
7. 117
8. truck
9. 4   783   21
10. 15, 16, 17

Exercise 67, pg. 71
1. 7:40 a.m.
2. A (1, 2)   B (4, 5)
3. 600
4. ray   angle
5. <
6. 2
7. 3
8. 6 or 2 and 3
9. 200   4179   5,894
10. square - 9 cm.
    triangle - 12 cm.
    hexagon - 6 cm.

Exercise 68, pg. 72
1. $4.04 $11.92
2. 8 cm.
3. shade 3 of the 5 parts
4. 2 hours and 45 minutes
5. 35,844   61
6. 3,912   1,909
7. answers will vary
8. answers will vary
9. <
10. 26 students

Exercise 69, pg. 73
1. $20 bill
2. possible number sentences:
   $5 \times 15 = 75$
   $15 \times 5 = 75$
   $75 \div 5 = 15$
   $75 \div 15 = 5$
3. right angle
   obtuse angle
   acute angle
4. 10 hot dogs
5. 31,452   31
6. circumference
7. 18,943   18,565
8. 4⁴⁄₁₀₀   4.06
9. 90
10. 4th grade

Exercise 70, pg. 74
1. 9th and 30th
2. 24th
3. yes
4. 6,189   3,187
5. 428 instead of 429
   rule - subtract 11
6. 1,314   15   8.32
7. 60 minutes
   30 minutes
   20 minutes
8. 618,236
9. 4/10   6/10   7/10   12/10
10. .6